DISTILLED IN
VERMONT

A History & Guide with Cocktail Recipes

CHRIS MAGGIOLO

Foreword by Jeremy Elliott
President of the Distilled Spirits Council of Vermont

AMERICAN PALATE

Published by American Palate
A Division of The History Press
Charleston, SC
www.historypress.com

Front cover, top right: Author Chris Maggiolo holds a handful of crushed rye grain. *Courtesy of SILO Distillery.*

First published 2020

Manufactured in the United States

ISBN 9781467141413

Library of Congress Control Number: 2020930486

Notice: The information in this book is true and complete to the best of our knowledge. It is offered without guarantee on the part of the author or The History Press. The author and The History Press disclaim all liability in connection with the use of this book.

To Laura
A Million Dreams, Forever and a Day

CONTENTS

Foreword, by Jeremy Elliott   7
Acknowledgements   9
Introduction   11

1. Ingredients: The Taste of Vermont   15

2. Production: From Farm to Flask   22

3. Maturation: Age Is More Than Just a Number   29

4. Packaging, Sales and Marketing: The Vermont Brand   36

5. Navigating the Control State   43

6. Dramatis Personae   48
   Appalachian Gap Distillery   48
   Caledonia Spirits   53
   Danger Close Craft Distilling   60
   Hell's Gate Distillery   63
   Hooker Mountain Farm Distillery   67
   Mad River Distillers   73
   Old Route Two Spirits   78
   Saxtons River Distillery   84

CONTENTS

Shelburne Orchards Distillery   88
SILO Distillery   93
Smugglers' Notch Distillery   98
St. Johnsbury Distillery   102
Stonecutter Spirits   108
Vermont Distillers   114
Vermont Spirits   117
WhistlePig Whiskey   120
Wild Hart Distillery   126

7. Cocktail Culture: A Gateway to Vermont Distilleries   132

8. Closing Thoughts   145

About the Distilled Spirits Council of Vermont   147
Notes   149
Bibliography   155
Index   157
About the Author   160

FOREWORD

When I reflect on the Vermont distilled spirits industry, I am proud of what we have accomplished and excited about our future. We are a thoughtful, vibrant, thriving group of entrepreneurs who collectively have managed to create something of the impossible, something that only dreams are made of. As Chris Maggiolo guides us through the distilled spirits journey in his book, it is important to remember and understand our roots. We are surrounded and inspired by fellow like-minded pioneers: cheese makers, maple syrup producers, craft beer manufacturers and many, many more. The passion for Vermont-made products is present and alive every day in our communities and beyond. That is what makes Vermont so special.

"Why start a distillery in Vermont?" is a question many of us get asked. It is a valid query since we are in one of the least populous states. For many, it is a connection with the land, the people and the idealism that Vermont is unique. I agree with all those and more. There is a sense of inspiration when you wake up and look over the mountains. There is a sense of aspiration when the first spring flowers arrive after a long, cold winter. These ideas or feelings are captured and bottled every day by our distilled spirits producers.

As the Vermont distilled spirits industry grows and morphs, it is important to chronicle our rapid growth. It was ten years ago before a Vermont distillery could offer tastes of its distilled spirits products to visitors to Vermont and locals interested in stopping by to say hello. It was eight years ago when we were recognized as a value-added agricultural industry to the farming community and allowed participation in farmers' markets. It was just four years ago when we were being taxed at a higher rate than any other business in Vermont, making growth impossible. Pivotal changes to help our industry flourish have taken place through a concerted effort from our industry members, believers and dreamers.

Personally, I am looking forward to this read. Chris Maggiolo has been "on the ground" in the Vermont distilled spirits industry by wearing several hats over the years: head distiller, consultant, active member of the Distilled Spirits Council of Vermont. He has not only witnessed our industry transformation but has been immersed in it firsthand. I encourage you to sit down, pour a bit of Vermont into your glass and enjoy this book.

—Jeremy Elliott
President/Co-Owner, Smugglers' Notch Distillery
President, Distilled Spirits Council of Vermont

ACKNOWLEDGEMENTS

Thank you to the Distilled Spirits Council of Vermont and to the numerous distillery owners and operators who took time from their busy schedules to entertain us with their stories.

Thank you to Patrick Delaney and his staff at the Department of Liquor and Lottery for insight into the life of the control state.

Thank you to all my friends and family who have supported me in this endeavor, especially my parents, Dan and Kim Maggiolo; my siblings, Steven, Samantha, Tyler and Rana; my other parents, Ron and Deb Kapushinski; and my other siblings, Brent and Chelsea.

Thank you to Ben and Sam of Flying Crow Coffee Co. for keeping me fueled and for giving me a place to write and to Nick and Elise of The Copper Fox for your cocktail inspirations and encouragement.

Finally, thank you to my wife, Laura, for believing in me and for relieving me from so many household responsibilities while I write. You continuously amaze me.

INTRODUCTION

Distillation is a story of agriculture and industry, of art and science, of man and machine. An incredibly old practice—some sources trace the origins of distillation to 500 BC India and Pakistan[1]—it is the essence of dichotomy and exotic mysticism. Indeed, the very process of distillation, the concept of heating and cooling to separate alcohol from a water-alcohol mixture, delves into themes of rebirth, yin and yang and the sum of parts.

Vermont's spirits industry is small but mighty. Its ever-expanding cast of characters represents everything from secluded farm distilleries to brands well known throughout the United States and beyond. A microcosm of the country's craft distilling movement, Vermont's distilling industry reflects the diverse techniques, motivations and products that can be found throughout the industry at large. Distillers open to discussing their craft freely comment on their businesses, their passions and their trials and tribulations.

I'll say it: by and large, there is a problem with the United States spirits industry and consumer education. Alcohol consumers simply don't understand the processes that bring their beloved products to their glasses. The craft beer movement did wonders for the world of beer, enlightening individuals on the finer points of brewing, hops and grain. The upfront, tactile experience of visiting a craft brewery, now found in nearly every small town, encourages consumers to explore: from the simplest of questions— "Hey, what's in this beer?"—to deep-seated desires resulting in volunteer hours, internships and even entrepreneurship.

In comparison, the spirits industry still rests within a veil of secrecy, behind the glass and beyond the red line. Craft distilleries work tirelessly to demystify spirits through tours, events and the inclusion of cocktail culture, but the deck is stacked against them. Unlike beer and wine, the idea of spirits—the "hard" stuff—remains closely associated with notions of alcoholism and crime, the same historic pattern that heralded the so-called Noble Experiment of national Prohibition.

"We use bombs to make drugs," one distiller said to me in an interview. And it's true. What we do can be dangerous, both while we do it and in its consumption. However, with the help of organizations dedicated to spirits legislation and consumption, and the perceived benefits of alcohol-related tourism, state governments are coming to understand the value generated by local and regional manufacturing. Still, many of the industry's finer points fly under the radar.

Riding the coattails of the American wine and craft beer industries, it is slowly becoming acceptable for beverage consumers to regularly enjoy a dram of whiskey, a Martini (shaken or stirred) or a simple gin and tonic. An upwelling of craft cocktail culture encourages the responsible consumption of spirits alongside meals. The resurgence of cocktails in the last decade is arguably the distilled spirits industry's greatest boon, an artful study of flavor and creative expression that is both routinely sought after and widely accepted.

When I tell people that I studied alcohol in college, they almost always laugh. "So did I!" is the most common response. Well, it's true. Raised in part by my French grandmother, I was always fascinated by wine, pastis[2] and, well…mostly wine. In college, I participated in archaeological digs and the study of the economic history of rum in the Caribbean. My first job after college was with the Williamsburg Winery, after which I moved to Boston to further study the anthropology of craft beer and spirits at Boston University.

My first real foray into craft distilling occurred in 2013 while traveling the country in the back of a twenty-year-old baby blue van. While conducting research for a capstone project, I became enamored of the art, science and intentionality of the fledgling spirits industry.[3] I returned home after three months and fifteen thousand miles on the road and immediately searched for an apprenticeship at a distillery. GrandTen Distilling in South Boston provided me an opportunity for hands-on experience, and I never looked back.

Taking a job as head distiller and production manager for SILO Distillery, I moved to Windsor, Vermont, in 2015. At SILO, I learned firsthand of

Vermont's unique position at the forefront of artisan food and beverage production. To this day, I am shocked at just how small of a state Vermont is.[4] The farmers who help feed SILO quickly became friends, introducing me to other grain producers, herb cultivators, sugaring operations and so much more. Even our legislators are but a phone call away—and they frequently answer their own phones!

When the opportunity struck to write this book, I jumped. I've always loved giving tours and tastings, loved the educational aspects of what we do. There's an amazing moment when talking about spirits—and boy, can I talk about spirits—when a process or flavor is described and a consumer's eyes widen. It sinks in, the dam springs a leak and questions pour forth. It's easy enough describing the first moments of grain-to-glass distilling. After all, it's much like brewing, and people are fairly familiar with beer. Take 1,600 gallons of beer and distill it down to 40 to 50 gallons of 80 proof spirit, and you've got a different story.

Distilled in Vermont is a field guide of sorts, a snapshot of distillery life in the Green Mountain State and an overview of what it takes to bring a raw product from concept to cocktail. No one chapter is exhaustive by any means—entire books can be, and indeed have been, written about each subject individually—but the contents should give readers a better understanding of the various labors of love that make up a distilled spirits product.

This book is divided into three parts. The first section outlines the distilling process: ingredients, distillation, maturation, marketing and Vermont's status as a control state. "Ingredients" highlights the products used to make spirits and features the work of Andrew Peterson and Peterson Quality Malt. "Maturation" introduces the veteran-owned-and-operated Green Mountain Grain & Barrel and the intricacies of barrel-aging. "Navigating the Control State" features a fascinating interview with Patrick Delaney, commissioner of Vermont's Department of Liquor and Lottery.

Section two is a dramatis personae, a directory of the main characters of our spirited story. Well over twenty distilled spirits plants (DSPs) exist in Vermont, with roughly twenty producing and selling product. As part of this project, I've had the distinct pleasure of interviewing seventeen of these producers, the distillery owners and operators responsible for Vermont's prospering distilling industry. The profiles highlighted in section two feature quotes from these interviews, preserving as much as possible the voices of those "on the ground" in the industry. Each profile illuminates both the featured distillery and core themes of the distilling industry, common to craft distillers everywhere.

Finally, Vermont distilleries and bartenders come together to offer a carefully curated selection of craft cocktail recipes. From simple mixed cocktails to artfully constructed creations, I hope that something sparks your interest!

Vermont's distilling industry is incredibly intricate—socially, technically and procedurally. It is my sincere hope that *Distilled in Vermont* helps shed light on the complex structure of spirits production while simultaneously generating excitement for the amazing community that calls Vermont home.

Chapter 1

INGREDIENTS

The Taste of Vermont

Whiskey is liquid sunshine.
—*George Bernard Shaw*

J ust like a home-cooked meal, the distillation of quality spirits begins with choosing the best ingredients for the job. In fact, most spirits are categorized directly by the types of ingredients used to produce or flavor them. Gin, for example, must incorporate juniper berries, which in turn produce the characteristic "pine tree" flavors and aromas for which it is known. Whiskeys are categorized by their predominant grain—corn, rye, wheat or barley. Rum isn't rum without its sugary base, and brandy is derived from fruit. Vermont's unique agricultural landscape favors small diversified farms and thus the cultivation of a wide variety of fruits, herbs, vegetables and other products suitable for distillation.

The history of grain production in Vermont is turbulent at best. Settled in 1724 by Massachusetts colonists, Fort Drummer—located in southern Vermont near modern Brattleboro—was the state's first permanent European settlement.[5] From there, colonists continued to push north into the Champlain Basin, where fertile soils and an ideal climate cultivated conditions perfect for growing wheat. Grain farming boomed. The production of wheat became so important that when Ira Allen, brother of Ethan Allen, designed the state seal in 1778, he included two shocks of wheat in the design.[6]

The state seal of Vermont, designed by Ira Allen, features natural and agricultural symbols.

Coupled with soil depletion from heavy cropping and crop loss due to pests, the completion of the Erie Canal in 1825 sounded the death knell for Vermont wheat production. Vermont quickly lost its status as breadbasket of New England as farms moved to the Genesee Valley of western New York, closer to the canal and new shipping hub. While wheat production in Vermont peaked at 644,000 bushels in 1840, by the turn of the century, only 35.65 bushels were harvested statewide.[7]

Andrew Peterson, founder of the rapidly growing Peterson Quality Malt malthouse, works hard to help revitalize regional grain-growing. Until now, most of the malted grain Andrew produces has come from within a ten-mile radius of his house and its attached malthouse, converted from an old dairy barn.[8]

Most of the grain currently comes from about ten miles of here. So we've got a little we do right here and we have fields we rent in the area. There's one family that we've started working with—two brothers who bought their grandparents' old dairy farm. They wanted to do grains. So it's really the perfect sort of partnership. They know what they're doing. They're great farmers. We have the same core values—putting up good rotations which are good for the soils, not avoiding the idea of contemplating runoff, so forth. They're really good guys.

With the help of Hotel Vermont, Peterson has recently acquired Nordic Farm in Charlotte, Vermont. His malting operation is poised to increase dramatically.

At Nordic we've got more acres than we had total around here. The total acreage at Nordic is 583. There's about 350 tillable. Last year we planted about 225. This year we'll get all the rest of it ready. And then we're leasing a bunch of land around there. Last year in the state we did about 720 acres total. Two years ago right around here we did 150. This year we're trying to get to 1,500 acres, and by 2023 we're trying for 7,000 acres.

Andrew Peterson, owner of Peterson Quality Malts. *Courtesy of Peterson Quality Malts.*

Andrew's malting process is time consuming. Starting on the second floor at a moisture level of 12 to 13 percent, grain is soaked on and off for several hours at a time until it reaches about 45 percent moisture content. At this point, the grain believes it has been planted and will start to grow. The sprouted grain is moved to germination tanks on the first floor, where it spends four days under carefully monitored humidity and temperature levels.

Andrew explains, "When it's done four days from now, it will be close to the top since the rootlets expand. Right now we mix with a canoe paddle. If you don't, it'll mat up into a giant brick. In the new place, it'll be done automatically with an augur that will go through it. At this size, we can do it with a paddle. At the new size, everyone would quit."

From the germination tanks, the sprouted malt is moved to the basement to be kiln dried. The temperature is raised to 150 to 160 degrees Fahrenheit as high volumes of air are blown through the grain. In a mere twenty-four hours, the moisture content will drop from 45 percent to 5 to 6 percent. It is now ready to be polished, separated and bagged.

So we're looking at expanding this infrastructure which the state hasn't had in 120 years. Some of that goes past grains for brewing—grains for distilling, food-grade grains, we're putting in a flaker for flaked grains and we're putting in a flour mill to produce wheat flour, rye flour, cornmeal and stuff like that. I wish someone else had come on and done this, but it's not there. So it's sort of on us to create potential. You can't have a farmer bring us grain, have us evaluate it and say, "Yeah, it's not good for us, so take it away." In the long run, farmers will say, "Yeah, this is too complicated. We need another outlet." So if someone comes in and their barley is terrible that year, we can always turn around and send it to the feed-grade division or something.

Barley and wheat aren't the only grains being grown in Vermont. At SILO Distillery, I worked closely with Jeff Grembowicz and Grembowicz Farm, a fourth-generation farm in North Clarendon, Vermont. Jeff and his father steward six hundred acres of crops, mostly corn. Originally a dairy farm, the Grembowicz family transitioned to diversified grain farming in 2005. The farm is the sole producer of the non-GMO corn and rye used by SILO in its farm-to-glass spirits.[9]

If there's anything Jeff and Andrew have taught me, it's that farming in Vermont is never a guaranteed endeavor. Sometimes, says Andrew, it's the climate:

Yes, you can go out west. Kansas, you pick the rain line that's perfect. You plan right along there, and you know exactly what you're going to get year after year. Vermont gets this rap as a bad growing state compared to places like that. There are good years and bad years. Heather Darby at the University of Vermont will say that two out of five years in Vermont are really good grain years. What happens to those other three? Sometimes they can be so-so years, and sometimes they can be really bad years. Two years ago, it was so wet that there were fields that we didn't even attempt to harvest.

At other times, you're at the whim of socioeconomics:

Finding growers initially was hard. For the most part, you're looking at farmers who are fairly conservative in their ways. They've heard people come along and say, "We'll pay you for this." We've seen farmers be offered ridiculous things they'll never see, things which will hurt them. For us, it was a couple years ago when dairy started crashing fast. Places that were getting out of dairy were doing hay and selling it to neighbors down the road who were still doing dairy. Now, two years have passed and the dairy guys

Production employees at Mad River Distillers unload a delivery of ingredients. *Courtesy of Mad River Distillers.*

haven't paid the hay guys because they have their own financial problems. So now let's look at this grain thing.

And so Vermont, spurred onward by the beer and spirits industries and ever the proponent of a do-it-yourself mentality, seeks a return to its glory as "New England's breadbasket."[10] This alone would paint a delightful picture of innovation and agricultural revitalization, but stories of wheat and barley are only the tip of the figurative iceberg. While grain is an undeniably important part of the distilling process, Vermont distillers have long tapped into numerous other agricultural products as well.

Maple syrup remains one of Vermont's most beloved icons. Indeed, it's hard to conceive of Vermont without its miles of sap lines and thousands of rustic sap buckets and sugar shacks. It's rather expected that several Vermont distilleries capitalize on the sweet pastime of sugaring, producing many maple-inspired liqueurs and flavored whiskeys or rums. Vermont Distillers' Metcalfe's Vermont Maple Cream Liqueur and Saxtons River Distillery's Sapling Maple Liqueur are two of the more ubiquitous, maple-forward spirits found in the Green Mountain State. As with these, most distilleries blend Vermont-made syrup with spirits to create sweet, easy-to-drink offerings that are incredibly popular with visitors and locals alike. Some distilleries are even more innovative. Appalachian Gap Distillery, for example, directly distills maple syrup and agave into Papilio, a unique spirit reminiscent of tequila.

One cannot talk about maple without mentioning its golden cousin, honey. Though Vermont is more frequently associated with the former rather than the latter, honey plays an important role in many of the state's distilleries. Caledonia Spirits is known for its honey-based portfolio, its award-winning products available throughout the United States and internationally. Todd Hardie, a lifelong beekeeper, began Caledonia Spirits after forty-eight years in the beekeeping world and brought with him a distinct passion for incorporating working landscapes and local agriculture into the Caledonia Spirits products.[11] Old Route Two Spirits, one of Vermont's newest distilleries, uses mead from Groennfell Meadery in Colchester, Vermont, to produce Viking Funeral, a unique honey spirit.

A number of fruits, vegetables and herbs are also utilized by Vermont's numerous distillers. Apples, while prolific in Vermont, appear infrequently in spirits due to the large quantities needed in order to produce a scalable product and the rather high cost of goods associated with quality cider fruit. Able to utilize its own apples for brandy production, Shelburne Orchards

Barr Hill celebrates bees, honey and agriculture. *Courtesy of Caledonia Spirits.*

Distillery is a notable exception. Mad River Distillers also produces an apple brandy in a limited quantity, while SILO Distillery uses apples as a secondary botanical in its gin. With the popularity of gin ever on the rise, a number of small farms have been contracted to cultivate herbs and other desirable botanicals, though juniper berries—the primary botanical component in all gins—are typically sourced regionally or nationally.

Vermont is known for its cottage industries, and Vermont distilleries share numerous qualities with these other self-starters. Equipment is frequently fabricated in-house, and ingredients are often sourced locally or regionally should a feasible option exist. Scalability tends to be the largest obstacle when committing to local supply chains, though companies such as Peterson Quality Malt work hard to meet the demands of both brewers and distillers alike. Once ingredients are sourced and received, production can begin. It's a labor-intensive, mechanical, industrial process, but one that truly blends the line between science and art.

Chapter 2

PRODUCTION

From Farm to Flask

Civilization begins with distillation.
—*William Faulkner*

Once a distiller selects ingredients for a product—grain for whiskey, fruit for brandy or perhaps even a nontraditional fermentable such as maple or honey—they can begin transforming those ingredients into the spirits that consumers know and love. Ingredients are first prepared for a mash and fermentation, typically by crushing, grinding and blending with water. The mash helps to convert starches into simple sugars, which are then fermented by yeast and/or bacteria into alcohol. Alcohol passes through the still in a series of distillations, producing the desired finished product.

Preparing an ingredient for fermentation and distillation is a messy job.[12] Raw and malted grains are typically milled before use in order to expose starches and proteins to enzymatic reactions. Grinding increases the grain's surface area and allows water and enzymes a better chance to penetrate the grain. Generally, a hammer mill is used to grind rye, wheat and corn; a roller mill is used for malted barley; and a cage mill is used for all four grains.[13]

Roller mills are frequently used by distillers who wish to produce malt whiskeys and are the same kind of mill used by brewers. The larger grist and intact husks result in grain that is more easily separated from liquid for off-the-grain distilling. The finer crush achievable by hammer and cage mills can lead to a more efficient distillation with a higher alcohol yield (more surface area means more starch conversion) but is more difficult to separate

Open-topped fermentation at Hooker Mountain Farm Distillery. *Courtesy of Hooker Mountain Farm Distillery.*

from liquids after a mash. As a result, spirits made from finer crushes are frequently fermented and distilled on-the-grain.

Mashing is the stage of malt distilling where ground, malted grain is mixed with water and heated to a specific temperature such that the starches gelatinize and enzymes are able to convert those starches into fermentable sugars. Mash temperatures for malted barley typically range from 145 to 158 degrees Fahrenheit. These sugars are dissolved into the water and are frequently separated from the grains, cooled and fermented.[14]

Grain distilling—the distillation of unmalted grains such as corn, wheat and rye—undergoes a process similar to mashing known as "cooking." The gelatinization temperatures of these grains are much higher than malted barley—167 degrees Fahrenheit for rye and wheat to as high as 194 degrees Fahrenheit for corn.[15] In most cases, grain distillers will add enzymes to help convert starches into sugars and to further help the gelatinization process.[16]

The malt and grains cook at their desired temperatures until starch conversion is complete, at which point the mash will be cooled to a temperature suitable for the addition of yeast. Distiller's yeast tends to be more aggressive than brewing yeast, fermenting hotter, faster and to a higher alcohol percentage, leaving little to no sugar behind. An incredibly important part of the process, fermentation is responsible for the production of numerous flavor compounds, frequently known as esters and congeners, which react to and influence the flavors in a finished spirit.[17]

Some producers cultivate their own mother batches of yeast, carefully guarding the culture as one would a prized, secret ingredient. Other distilleries purchase distinct yeast cultures from one of several laboratories. Once yeast is added, the mash can be transferred to a fermenter to undergo fermentation, the process whereby yeast convert sugars into ethyl alcohol and carbon dioxide.

So what is distillation, exactly? In a nutshell, distilling is the process of concentrating or separating parts of a liquid using boiling and condensation. In the case of spirits, we boil a fermented liquid in order to separate the alcohol from the water, thereby concentrating the alcohol percentage. Ethanol and other alcohols have lower boiling points than water—about 173 degrees Fahrenheit for ethanol compared to 212 degrees Fahrenheit for water.

As you heat up a liquid containing both ethanol and water, the ethanol will boil off first. As the temperature rises, more alcohol will boil off as well as some water, and the vapor will be condensed back into a liquid through a cooler condensing column. Distillers rarely handle 100 percent ethanol, but it's fairly common to work with product as high as 95 percent alcohol-by-volume (ABV) and anywhere lower.

The stills by which one distills vary in size and shape, largely indicative of the products a company wishes to produce. Generally speaking, and there are certainly exceptions, pot stills are used to produce scotch, mezcal, rum, brandy and other spirits where the end goal is a more flavorful product. A fermented wash is placed in a large, bulbous pot and is heated, directly or indirectly via a jacket. As the product reaches a boil, it evaporates and travels into a condensing column to cool and return to liquid form. Pot stills do not achieve as efficient a separation of alcohol, water and flavor compounds, resulting in a more flavorful finished spirit. After each run on the still, the still must be cleaned out and prepared for the next distillation.

By comparison, column stills are often used to produce vodka, dry gins, white rums and spirits where a distinctly clean, less flavor-forward finish is desired. Many mainstream bourbons and rye whiskeys are also produced with column stills, using a "continuous still" to increase throughput while minimizing downtime. Imagine, if you will, a tall column composed of several chambers and heated from the bottom. Each chamber is essentially a small still. The wash, low in ABV, enters at the top of the column

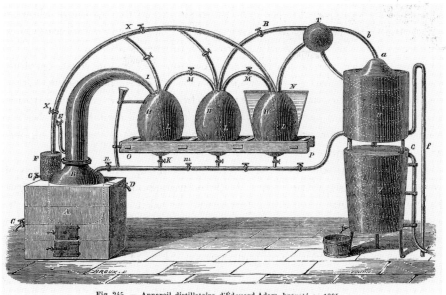

Fig. 245. — Appareil distillatoire d'Édouard Adam, breveté en 1805.

A model of a historic still, circa 1805.

and begins to sink. It interacts with the heated base of the column and vaporizes, rising back up.

As the vapor hits the top of a chamber, it condenses much like water vapor on the bottom of a pot lid. The heavier compounds fall, and the lighter alcohol compounds continue rising to the next chamber. Eventually, the alcohol sheds off all unnecessary weight (usually as water and congeners, or flavor compounds) and makes its way to the top of the highest chambers, where it passes to the condensing column and returns to its liquid state. The end product tends to be much higher in ABV and largely without the flavor compounds present at the end of a pot still distillation.

In the contemporary distilling industry, many craft distilleries run a hybridized version of these two styles. In most hybrid stills, a pot is used to heat the mash, and depending on the spirit being produced, the vapor may or may not be channeled into a column. This gives the smaller craft distillery the ability to produce a variety of spirit types rather than focusing on a chosen few.

Though a technical skill grounded in scientific methodology, the act of distillation retains a certain amount of artistic finesse. Every distiller has his or her own style, own beliefs and brushstrokes for creating the "perfect"

SILO Distillery production floor, featuring Christian Carl still. *Courtesy of SILO Distillery.*

product. Some distillers will distill a finished product using only a single pass through a still, believing it to be more flavorful and textured. Others will utilize a step called a "stripping run" in order to increase the efficiency of the process and purity of the finished product. In a stripping run, the wash is run quickly through the still. The alcohol is concentrated to about 35 to 40 percent ABV, and all compounds, good and bad, remain in the product. Pungent, oily and rough, the spirit at the end of the stripping run is frequently called "low wines."

Low wines can be collected over the course of many stripping runs and are eventually placed back into the still for what's known as the "finish run" or "spirit run": the distillation used to produce a clean, finished product. As the finish run occurs, it is the distiller's job to determine the "cuts"—which parts of the final product will be kept and which will be discarded. Cuts can be broken into four distinct categories: foreshots, heads, hearts and tails.

Foreshots represent the first vapors to be boiled off and condensed and contain poisonous compounds such as methanol. They feel cold and dry, much like rubbing alcohol, and compose 5 percent or less of the finish run. Every distiller discards these; nobody likes poison.

As the foreshots subside, the heads come into play. Characterized by unpalatable flavors, sharpness, bitterness and astringency, heads aren't much better than foreshots. Made up of lighter compounds such as acetone (found in some nail polish removers), acetaldehyde and acetate, the heads cut of a finish run is said to be one of the primary causes of a bad hangover. About 20 to 30 percent of a finish run will be heads and can be discarded.

The heart of the run is the sweet spot. Hearts have the purest ethanol. The sharpness and bitterness of the heads has passed, leaving a sweet, smooth and flavorful core. Hearts compose 30 to 40 percent of the finish run, and it's a distiller's job to know when to start and stop collecting this important cut. Most distillers use a combination of gauges, temperature readings, alcohol readings and sensory analysis (taste, smell and touch) in order to determine the heart cut.[18]

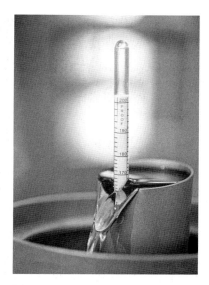

Hydrometer in parrot during whiskey run, measuring proof. *Courtesy of SILO Distillery.*

Tails make up the last 20 to 30 percent of the finish run and are primarily made of less volatile alcohols, oils, proteins and carbohydrates. They lack the smoothness and sweetness of the hearts, instead tasting thin and feeling slick. In fact, the oils may even separate from the spirit to show an oily sheen atop the liquid. Sometimes a distiller will keep the tails, combining them with the wash of a future run in order to distill every last drop of flavor. Tails kept in this way are frequently referred to as feints.

Once a base spirit has been distilled, it can travel down many paths. If the distillery is producing regular vodka, the spirit can be cut with water (a step called "proofing") to bottle strength and filtered until it is ready to be bottled. Flavored vodkas and gins, however, require additional steps in order to properly infuse them with flavors. These steps could be cold infusions similar to steeping a tea bag, or they could be an additional distillation. Different botanicals react to alcohol and heat in different ways. Some benefit by soaking in ethanol and undergoing a quick distillation in order to harvest their flavors. Others are too delicate and are instead placed in a "gin basket," a porous chamber placed in the path of the distillation vapors. As the vapors pass through the gin basket on their way to the condenser, they pull the flavor of the botanicals with them. The finished gin should rest for some time in order to reach an equilibrium with all its new flavors and can then be bottled per usual.

Whiskey and other dark spirits usually forego the bottling stage at this time, destined instead to spend time in oak barrels or similar cooperage. All spirits leave the still as clear as water. It is the prolonged contact with wood that gives aged whiskey, rum, tequila and brandy their characteristically dark hue. Barrel maturation not only provides color but also produces many of the key flavor components for which these spirits are known.

Chapter 3

MATURATION

Age Is More Than Just a Number

An Oak tree is a daily reminder that great things often have small beginnings.
—Matshona Dhliwayo

Barrels have long been the most common storage vessels for liquids. The process of forming a barrel shape from staves was known to ancient Egyptians and was used heavily throughout ancient Rome.[19] Kings Henry VIII and George III set several mandates that governed legal barrel capacities dependent on contents and geographical location. Some of these barrel sizes are still recognized today and bear unique names: rundlet, firkin, hogshead, butt and puncheon, to name a few.[20] While most spirits were historically consumed as "new make," unmatured spirits, it was eventually discovered that spirits matured in barrels benefited from enhanced flavors and aromas.

Aged spirits are commonplace among Vermont distilleries. Indeed, WhistlePig Whiskey and Stonecutter Spirits have built strong reputations as stewards of maturation and barrel aging, bringing home several prestigious awards in the process. Other distilleries such as Caledonia Spirits, SILO Distillery and Old Route Two Spirits have made commitments to using local and regional cooperages for barrel production.[21] Quality barrels are highly sought after, and national cooperages frequently implement waiting lists, minimum order sizes and down payments months to years in advance. Army veterans Tony Fletcher, Mac Broich and Josh Waterhouse recognized the growing demand for barrels among Vermont distilleries,

Left to right: Tony Fletcher, Josh Waterhouse and Mac Broich. *Courtesy of Green Mountain Grain & Barrel.*

wineries and breweries and in 2016 founded Green Mountain Grain & Barrel to support these local producers.

Green Mountain Grain & Barrel sources 80 to 100 percent of its oak from Vermont, with the remainder being sourced regionally from locations such as New York or Connecticut.[22] Oak, the ideal wood for barrel production, makes up only a miniscule fraction of Vermont's annual hardwood harvest. As a result, the cooperage has partnered with other Vermont timber companies to ensure access to a local supply.

A considerable amount of work is required in order to transform oak logs into watertight barrels. Quarter sawn wood is delivered to the cooperage, where it is seasoned for at least two years. Mac explains, "The seasoning process…it softens the tannins. Everyone that burns wood for their house, no matter what species, they let it sit for a year. That just naturally lets the wood get less harsh in the form of tannins."

Tony adds, "Chemically, it changes it. There's a lot of bacterial stuff that goes on, and that's what breaks down those tannins. It's a chemical, biological change."

Staves are brought inside the cooperage and are further dried until they reach the desired moisture level. They are cut down to width and then run through a planer. "If there's a knot right in the middle or on an end, we'll cut it off and stick it in the stack for heads. Otherwise, it'll make its way through the planer and it'll get stacked here, where we'll have it for stave stock. Then it's ready for the big momma."

The "big momma" is a Ledineck stave jointer, a large piece of machinery designed to quickly and accurately produce barrel staves. Mac notes, "The tools that we were using to do all this were just modified homeowner shop-ish kind of tools." Before the arrival of the Ledineck, made possible by a grant from the Vermont Agency of Agriculture, the Green Mountain Grain & Barrel team could produce one stave every five minutes. Now, with the help of the stave jointer, they can produce one stave every twenty-three seconds. "Tony wasn't even racing, but was like, 'Hey, I just made a hundred staves.' It only took him forty minutes. Before, one hundred staves would have been a week. Run to the shop, get more blades and everything."

The staves are arranged in a skirt shape and are moved to a small bending room. A fire is built in a cresset (a cooperage tool similar in shape and function to a charcoal chimney starter), and the skirt of staves is placed over the heat source. A wet cloth is continuously applied to the wood to keep it damp and flexible, and a winch draws a cable tight around the skirt to bend it into the traditional barrel shape. The shaping process takes approximately an hour, though Tony hopes that a larger cresset can cut that time in half.

It's also toasting the inside at the same time that it's warming it up. Caramelizing the sugars, softening the tannins a little bit, doing some of that chemistry before it's actually charred. If it's a wine barrel or cider barrel we'd leave it like that, just toasted. This is an assembly hoop. Once it's tight enough, we'll place this over the top of it, and this temporarily holds it while we put the rest of the hoops in place.

Mac adds, "Then you let it cool into position and kind of bang out the middle to get it that nice bell shape. Then you keep it bell shaped and let it cool and continue on with finishing it up."

While winemakers and many cidermakers tend to prefer a toasted barrel, spirits tend to mature within charred oak barrels. The next step, therefore, is to take the unfinished barrel outside and light the interior on fire. Tony explains, "We then use a driveway blowtorch to ignite the center on fire. It's fully ignited for probably a full minute. Right at that point when you're starting to get scared it won't go out—that's when you put it out."

The barrel is nearly done. The staves are set in the correct shape and the barrel heads are ready to be placed. Tony details the finishing touches:

For the head we use a dowel method. We drill holes, we hammer a dowel in and we make the boards fit together. We cut it into a circle. We cut the inside

A skirt of staves and an unfinished barrel. *Courtesy of Green Mountain Grain & Barrel.*

Tony chars a barrel with a backyard flamethrower. *Courtesy of Green Mountain Grain & Barrel.*

of the croze out. Up here on the bottom left, that's an old cooperage croze. We modeled ours after that. We took a router and modeled that shape. So we run that around the inside and it cuts out a groove. We measure around the inside and cut out the head to fit it. Sometimes one head might be slightly smaller or bigger than the other so we do each one individually.

With the barrel heads secured, the team uses beeswax from Caledonia Spirits to seal the seams. The hoops are carefully secured with screws, the barrel heads are branded with the GMG&B stamp and the finished product heads to a Vermont distillery to be filled.

What happens to a spirit when it sits in a barrel? The answer is a complex one. On the surface, most readily observed, the barrel-aging process imparts color to a spirit. As noted earlier, the distillation process renders a spirit as clear as pure water. Color must be reintroduced to a product; many mass-produced spirits use caramel coloring and other artificial and natural additives to produce consistent colors, while numerous post-distillation botanical infusions contribute their own hues. Barrel-aging transforms a clear spirit into a brown or amber spirit. For example, white whiskeys, light rums and clear tequilas are all converted into their darker, more mature selves.

The beauty of an aged spirit is not just skin deep. Even a short amount of time in a barrel ignites a series of intricate chemical reactions, adding further depth and character to a product's flavor profile and structure. Typically, the longer a distilled spirit rests in a barrel, the more character it unveils. Furthermore, many products must be produced according to distinct aging parameters. American bourbon whiskey, for example, must be aged in new, charred oak barrels.[23] Other whiskeys may rest in used bourbon barrels, used sherry casks or other previously used cooperage. Though it takes more planning and capital to produce mature spirits, the high consumer demand for barrel-aged products demonstrates a preference for mature spirits over their new make versions.

There are many reasons why oak is the primary wood used for barrel construction, chief among them related to structural integrity and the development of flavor components. Certain structural components in oak contribute to its strength and flexibility, which in turn aid in the coopering process. Tannins present in oak provide astringency and structure to a whiskey while also removing unpleasant sulphurous flavors and helping to break down lignin. Lignin, an organic molecule responsible in part for the wood's rigidity, breaks down over time into aromatic compounds that contribute to floral notes as well as smoke, clove and vanilla.[24]

The process of barrel charring helps to naturally filter and polish the spirit and also breaks down hemicellulose, another structural component present in the wood. Hemicellulose contains numerous sugars and is easily broken apart when heated. When charred, these sugars transform into a number of aromatic congeners and are responsible for flavors such as almond, walnut, caramel, malt and maple.[25]

Charring also acts as a catalyst for oxidation. As a barrel's contents penetrate the wood through the charred interior surface, they interact with and react to atmospheric oxygen. Several unwanted volatile components present in the spirit will dissipate over time while other compounds are softened, enhanced or otherwise changed as the spirit matures.[26]

Not all oak is created equal, and there is still much to be learned about Vermont-grown oak. Green Mountain Grain & Barrel has recently started working with the University of New Hampshire in order to demystify its locally sourced wood. Tony explains:

> *There's something different about Vermont oak. It ages more slowly. We're using wood from Vermont. There's definitely a tighter grain. We don't specifically know that that is the reason. We're working with the UNH extension forestry division, and they're going to do a chemical analysis of the wood. They're working with Seguin Moreau cooperage in France to analyze it and run it through the spectrometer to see how it's different from Missouri oak, from Kentucky oak. We're excited to see those differences.*

The information gleaned from a study on Vermont oak and its properties will be an invaluable tool for Vermont distilleries, providing priceless insight into how barrels produced using Vermont oak may influence the spirits matured within them.

Finally, the maturation process cannot be discussed without mentioning loss—that is, the loss of volume over time while maturing. In the United States, whiskey barrels must be filled at no greater than 125 proof (62.5 percent ABV).[27] This limit reflects the generally higher temperatures and lower relative humidity found in our aging warehouses as compared to those of other whiskey-producing countries. In these conditions, water will evaporate and leave the barrel before ethanol, resulting in a higher-strength spirit in the cask. In cooler, more humid environments such as the United Kingdom, evaporative losses of ethanol are greater than those of water. Barrels tend to be filled at a higher proof to prevent the increased loss of ethanol over time from degrading the structure and quality of the spirit.

The evaporated contents of a barrel are frequently referred to as the "angel's share." In the UK, losses amount to 1 to 2 percent of total volume per year. In India or Australia, this can reach as high as 12 percent per year.[28] With the average summer high in Vermont sitting around eighty degrees Fahrenheit (compared to Scotland's average high in the low sixties), Vermont distillers experience a higher level of evaporation and a quicker rate of maturity than our UK counterparts. An angel's share of 3 to 4 percent is expected, with higher amounts in the first year as the freshly barreled spirit is absorbed into the barrel's wood. As the temperature and humidity fluctuate over the course of months and years, the barrel and its contents will expand and contract. This "breathing" in and out of the wood contributes to the spirit's maturation and growth in complexity and structure.

Maturation is expected to occur more rapidly in smaller cask sizes, especially with regard to evaporation and chemical reactions that depend on surface contact between the spirit and barrel. Most craft distilleries use smaller barrels—ten-, fifteen- and thirty-gallon formats—as a way of producing mature-tasting spirits in a fraction of the time it takes to produce a mature spirit in a "common" fifty-three-gallon barrel. While a spirit may take four to six years or considerably longer to mature in a fifty-three-gallon barrel, distillers may utilize a smaller barrel to achieve the idea of a similar product in as little as ten months to a year.[29] While color and certain congeners, especially those introduced by charring, will quickly react with a young spirit, other components of a premium well-aged spirit require years to fully develop. Many young distilleries, including those in Vermont, utilize small-format barrel programs in order to quickly release aged product and stabilize cash flow while working on, or intending to work on, a full-format barrel program for future releases.

The aging process is incredibly complex and is dependent on the makeup of the maturing spirit, the physical and chemical properties of the cask, the duration of maturation and the conditions of the cask's aging environment. It is a costly process, both in quantities of time and financial capital, and as such requires considerable attention and care. For many smaller craft distilleries, barrel programs grow organically as the distillery grows, tended by the staff at hand. Others recognize the need for a targeted maturation plan and may even hire a master blender or cellar master as steward of the aging process. Regardless of method, distillers recognize the value of aged spirits and their position at the vanguard of a fast-growing craft spirits industry.

Chapter 4

PACKAGING, SALES AND MARKETING

The Vermont Brand

Vermont is a jewel state—small but precious.
—Pearl S. Buck

Fermentation, distillation and maturation make up only part of a distilled spirit's life cycle. Bottles must also be labeled and filled, then marketed, distributed and sold. While not as exotic as distilling proper, these are invaluable pieces of a distilling business. On a store's shelf, eye-catching labels and unique bottle shapes and sizes draw in consumers long before the contents of the same bottle hit said consumers' lips.

The government-run Alcohol and Tobacco Tax and Trade Bureau (commonly referred to as the TTB) oversees the taxation and regulatory control of distilled spirits here in the United States. The TTB not only requires distilleries to submit recipes for many products, ensuring that distilled spirits are safe for consumption, but it also requires distilleries to submit product labels for review.[30] Labels must legibly indicate brand name, alcohol content, net contents and country of origin, and they must include a health warning statement.[31] A label must also denote the spirit's TTB class and type (such as vodka, whiskey, rum and so on), a regulatory designation built around the processes and ingredients used to produce a specific spirit type.

Net contents of a distilled spirits container must use metric units. Bottles range in size from nips (50 milliliters) to roughly a half gallon (1.75 liters) but have to be from a selection of specific volumes: 50 milliliters, 100 milliliters,

Department of the Treasury
Alcohol & Tobacco Tax & Trade Bureau

THE BEVERAGE ALCOHOL MANUAL (BAM)

A Practical Guide

Basic Mandatory Labeling Information For
DISTILLED SPIRITS

VOLUME 2

TTB P 5110.7 (04/2007)

Left: The TTB *Beverage Alcohol Manual* outlines "Class" and "Type" designations and limits how a product can be produced and labeled. *Tax and Trade Bureau, United States.*

Below: Labels may be applied manually or using semiautomatic or automatic machines. *Courtesy of Caledonia Spirits.*

200 milliliters, 375 milliliters, 750 milliliters, 1 liter and 1.75 liters. Spirits products sold in cans must be filled to 50 milliliters, 100 milliliters, 200 milliliters or 355 milliliters.[32] No other sizes are accepted.

Exploring the bottle industry can be an intimidating task. Many manufacturers are based overseas, though a few remain in the United States or maintain domestic plants. Bottles can be round, ovular, square or nonstandard in shape. Glass can be clear or tinted, screen-printed or frosted. Next come the industry-specific questions: Is the bottle shaped and weighted such that it can be easily handled and is bartender-friendly? Will the opening fit a pourer? Will it be easy to fill and label? Most craft distilleries, even the larger ones in Vermont, still bottle and label by hand, using semiautomatic bottle fillers and often affixing labels one at a time.

Distribution varies from distillery to distillery, as do marketing strategies. Some of Vermont's larger brands have near-nationwide distribution and distribute internationally, while others may just be selling from the distillery or investigating in-state distribution with the Vermont Division of Liquor Control (DLC). Whether selling in multiple markets or producing and selling straight from the farm, most Vermont distilleries brand themselves as champions of craftsmanship and artisanship. Some promote their grain-to-glass production processes, while others leverage the Vermont brand and the cultural capital of a terroir-like designation of origin.

Does Vermont have a distinct brand? In 2010, Vermont's chief marketing officer teamed up with the Department of Tourism and the Vermont Ski Area Association and delved into the subject.[33] In the related presentation, titled "Leveraging the Vermont Brand," the team quotes an 1891 promotion of Vermont: "A place of rural beauty, a place where farms produce wholesome food and where mountains, lakes and trails offer vigorous, refreshing outdoor recreation, a place where history is important and relationship to the land still means something."[34]

Focusing largely on vacationers and tourism, the report establishes ways in which Vermont businesses might differentiate Vermont products within competitive markets. Target consumers self-identify as adventurous, outdoorsy, spontaneous, thrifty, independent and idealistic. Surveyed consumers categorize Vermont as authentic, community-driven, pure and simple.[35] Even today, the most frequently identified physical symbols of Vermont parallel those suggested by the late nineteenth-century advertisement. Farmland, forests, mountains, streams and lakes dominate the state's visual iconography and that of its many producers.

Well known for its quality and diversity, Vermont's food and beverage industry mimics many of the sentiments outlined in the state's study. Spearheaded largely by Vermont brewers and cheesemakers, producers have cultivated a thriving and passionate community of consumers, the likes of which travel from far and wide to sample Vermont-made provisions. High-quality restaurants pop up in the smallest of Vermont villages, in highly acclaimed bed-and-breakfast lodgings and are peppered throughout cultural hubs such as Burlington, Stowe and Middlebury.

Sam Nelis, beverage director for Caledonia Spirits and president of the Green Mountain chapter of the United States Bartenders' Guild (USBG), has witnessed a similar evolution in Vermont spirits and cocktail culture.[36]

I think that [Vermont's] food culture is ahead of most of the country. People say that Vermont was green before green was cool. I would say that the cocktail culture, in a way, lagged behind a little bit. I'd say it really got started—the renaissance happened mostly in New York City in the early 2000s. Here, it was about ten years behind. Which is about normal, I'd say. Vermont was able to catch up very quickly to the cocktail renaissance because the vocabulary of fresh, real food, slow food, craft beer was already there.

He continues:

The respect for the food industry in Vermont is already so engrained, it carried over so quickly into craft beer which is what we're world-famous for. It was just a hop, skip and a jump from there to having people respect the craft of cocktails. Using both of those things—local spirits, local produce, local ingredients as much as possible—they started to realize that people could have a craft cocktail. Vermonters pick it up quickly.

For distillers, the Vermont brand holds weight in the Northeast, in New England and perhaps down to the mid-Atlantic. Farther afield, however, the value of "Vermont" wanes as the importance of broader themes and personal branding increases.

As both the co-founder of Smugglers' Notch Distillery and the president of the Distilled Spirits Council of Vermont, Jeremy Elliott was at first surprised when Vermont products didn't have quite the name recognition he expected.[37]

You know, starting this business here I thought Vermont would have a larger name or more recognition, but as we've grown nationally, and as some of my other competitors in the state have grown nationally, as soon as it leaves New England, the Vermont name is not nearly as powerful. I was out west recently for a conference. We were talking about Vermont and Vermont beer, and I mentioned Heady Topper. Nobody knew what that was. To us, Heady Topper is the ultimate [Vermont beer], right? At least as far as what people know. But people outside of New England don't even know what it is. I do think that the Vermont name conjures up a certain grandeur. I think that's why people vacation here and why we live here: mountains, snow, pure water, sort of a different, free lifestyle. But I think that picture only pertains to New England.

At Caledonia Spirits, another widely distributed Vermont distillery, Ryan Christiansen finds that while "Vermont" lends a powerful advantage, it may not strictly be Vermont-the-brand that people recognize, but rather the central, more abstract themes of the Vermont brand: agriculture, artisanship

Gravity-fed bottlers can fill several bottles at once from a hopper. *Courtesy of Caledonia Spirits.*

and the like. It's up to the distillery, then, to connect these core tenets back to the Vermont name. Caledonia Spirits keeps Vermont at the forefront of its product line. "Landcrafted® in the Heart of Vermont" is proudly printed on the label of its flagship Barr Hill Gin.[38]

"I think Vermont is our greatest asset," says Ryan.

I think there are places where it's underappreciated, but there are pockets. People think Vermont is a curious story. For example, I've spent a good amount of time in Dallas. I don't find Vermont resonates all that huge in Dallas. But in Napa Valley, California, it's amazing. You'd think, "This is wine country, they drink wine." Well, they speak agriculture. So we're telling an agricultural story. I find I don't have to overcome the importance of pollinators. They already know the importance of pollinators. They're probably contracting pollinators to come in and pollinate their vineyards. If they resonate with our mission, it's an easy win. If they don't, it may not be win-able. So it's very neighborhood-driven. But usually when they understand Vermont, I'm saying that these are my friends.

Branding is at work all the time. Sivan Cotel of Stonecutter spirits cautions against relying too heavily on the Vermont brand, a valuable reminder that a company's own brand is of paramount importance.[39]

The value of the Vermont brand is that they see Vermont on your sign and say, "Oh cool, Vermont. Tell me what you do." You still have to tell them what you do. I've found the Vermont brand kind of frustrating at times only because how important people think it is. I'm glad to have it. It's very important to us. It's part of who we are. But it doesn't make anything easier. It's frustrating how important people think it is because they place a weird focus on it here, locally. I can tell you most assuredly that when we go elsewhere and talk about ourselves, Vermont is one aspect among many.

Sivan remarks that Vermont's reputation for quality alcohol production slots very well into the larger social trend toward quality-consumed over quantity-consumed.

What we have found, expanding the Vermont brand part a bit, is that Vermont has a good reputation in alcohol. We have a fantastic beer scene, a fantastic spirits scene, a fantastic cider scene. We're starting to have a fantastic wine scene. That's really cool because we are firing on all cylinders. And that part has a really cool overlap because the way people consume alcohol in 2018 is not how they consumed alcohol fifty years ago. Someone who drinks good beer probably also drinks good whiskey. Not all the time, but they're probably at least interested. Someone who is interested in cider is probably also interested in beer or wine or spirits.

The trend toward a multifaceted consumer is reflected in the widespread diversification of distributor portfolios. Many businesses that once specialized in wine or beer sales now seek out emerging distilleries, hoping to secure distribution rights before competitors do so. Similarly, national and multinational beverage companies hungrily eye potential acquisitions. As one of seventeen control states throughout the country, Vermont remains somewhat insulated from the hyper-competitive environment of private distribution. For the most part, Vermont's control state model benefits the numerous craft distilleries that call the state home, providing them an accessible and stable sales outlet. As the state system continues to evolve, it does so while keeping in mind that the Vermont brand also applies to its eighty or so retail stores.[40]

Chapter 5

NAVIGATING THE CONTROL STATE

*We're lucky to be in a small state, to have direct contact with our legislators who
believe in us and believe we bring people to Vermont.*
—*Jeremy Elliott, president of Smugglers' Notch Distillery*

With the repeal of Prohibition in 1933, the powers that be restructured
alcohol distribution into a three-tier system, partially or entirely
prohibiting a single entity from owning the production, distribution
and retail divisions of a beverage alcohol supply chain. The Twenty-First
Amendment, responsible for the repeal, also granted states the right to self-
regulate the specifics of the three-tier system. As a result, states adopted
various levels of control.[41]

Most states adopted a license system, allowing retailers to purchase a
license from the state government for the retail of controlled substances
such as alcohol and tobacco. Vermont, along with sixteen other states
and Montgomery County, Maryland, operates instead as a control state.
Under the control state model, a state government assumes possession of
controlled substance products at some point between manufacturing and
retail to consumers. In the case of Vermont, this occurs when product leaves
the state warehouse on a delivery truck. Products remain the property of
the state until sold by one of Vermont's retail locations, whereby the state
recoups revenue.[42]

Patrick Delaney, commissioner of the Vermont Department of Liquor and Lottery (DLL), explains that the primary goal of the control state is to

create an acceptable balance between commercial interests and public safety interests. We license retailers. We select retailers. We establish pricing. We establish hours of operation. We maintain an acceptable balance point between population base and points of distribution. We work closely with local governments to ensure that their communities have a proper balance from their perspective in terms of accessibility and some of the potential negative effects of consumption. A public safety component is at the forefront of everything that we do.

He continues:

It's important to understand that our social mission is to encourage responsible behavior, to mitigate some of the negative outcomes of the misuse and abuse of alcohol. From a business standpoint, we are full-on a business within state government. No ifs, ands or buts about it. We are bottom-line oriented. The administration of this department today is focused on efficiencies, increasing levels of productivity and investing in levels of technology to have a better return on investments to the taxpayers of the state. It's important to understand that we do, in fact, compete against a neighboring state that has no excise tax and no sales tax.

While New Hampshire is also a control state, its model is noticeably different than Vermont's control state model. Rather than licensed agencies run by franchisees, a procedural shift that occurred in Vermont between 1986 and 1996, New Hampshire continues to run its own retail stores. An expensive endeavor, it allows for complete control of the system, investments in palatial retail outlets and an expansive inventory that includes wine alongside liquor. Both states commit net revenues to their respective general funds.[43]

"We'll generate about $27 million to the state's general fund this year. We generated $25 million last year. We generated $23 million in the 2017 fiscal year. The business is growing consistently."[44]

Vermont recognizes the value that local producers bring to the state, offering certain incentives for Vermont-based manufacturers. Local manufacturers have carte blanche, more or less, for initial product listings. The state pays COD for local products rather than holding them in bailment,

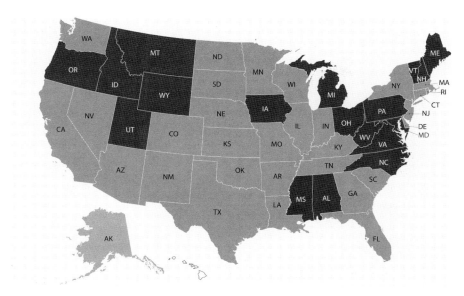

Active alcoholic beverage control states in the United States. *Courtesy of National Alcohol Beverage Control Association (NABCA).*

paying for them when they leave the warehouse. Local manufacturers may also retail their own products in their own establishments without needing to purchase their products from a state store.

"Basically," notes Delaney, "just about all of our other expectations apply unilaterally between local and nonlocal manufacturers. We have delisting criteria. If a product doesn't sell, we're not going to sell it. We don't have a one-size-fits-all expectation for continued listings. We've created an artificially low standard to allow local manufacturers additional wiggle room. Once again, if it doesn't reach that level, we have to do what we have to do. We have a responsibility to the citizens of the state, the legislature, as well as the manufacturers."

The Department of Liquor and Lottery works closely with legislators to evaluate and maintain the rules, regulations, policies and procedures of Title VII, the state's legal framework for the distribution and sale of controlled substances. Legislators recently updated Title VII—written in the 1930s after the repeal of Prohibition—in 2017. Updates included the modernization of language, the elimination of redundancies and the evaluation of penalties for noncompliance.

In addition to the DLL and legislators, the Distilled Spirits Council of Vermont (DSCVT), a coalition of distillery owners and operators largely focused on legislative change, explores revisions and amendments from the perspective of a manufacturer. The council promotes one or two legislative changes each session. Among their most recent undertakings is a proposed adjustment to an existing tax cliff.[45]

Ryan Christiansen, president of Caledonia Spirits, explains:

> The cliff is the most important thing. As currently written, there's a certain threshold, and if we cross that threshold, we pay tax. It's an incremental tax increase, which is fine. At certain thresholds it goes from 5 percent to 10 percent to 25 percent, but when you cross that 25 percent threshold you go back to every bottle sold in the period and pay 25 percent. From a business planning standpoint, it's impossible. I've done the math. There could come a time this year, should Barr Hill cross a certain threshold, that we'll have to pay $140,000 in tax on one $35 bottle sold.[46]

Ryan is confident that the issue will be resolved, likely before the printing of this book.

> It's literally in committee right now, happening right now. Patrick [Delaney] and the DLL are very supportive. Everyone wants to fix it. It's a matter of mechanics and how do we fix it. That's another attribute of the state of Vermont that's nice. You can call the commissioner and say, "I have a problem. Can we talk about it?" The DLL is very approachable. Our legislators are very approachable. I love the smallness of Vermont, and I hope we can retain the smallness of Vermont. I also love that legislators are looking at these small brands as tourism-drivers and a real opportunity of advertising.

Brendan Hughes, president of St. Johnsbury Distillery, cites the logistical benefits of a control state rather than legislative changes.[47]

> The state's very helpful, especially as a control state. I love the aspect that you only have to work with one location. When you work with a non-control state, it's a bit more ambiguous working on the delivery side and everything like that. It's nice to have that central location in Montpelier that you can deliver to. They do a great job in feeding us numbers, as well—giving us our levels before we need to restock and such. They're definitely helpful. Getting started, too, being able to bounce questions off of them. Going through the process now of opening up a new facility, being able to have an open channel of communication is definitely helpful.

Increasing communication efforts and efficiency has been a focal point of the DLL's administrative office. Until a recent overhaul, many state agencies were far too isolated from the main office. Several outlets still managed to limp along using archaic dial-up equipment and snail mail rather than integrated electronic systems. Delaney's office has worked hard to address these issues, among others.

Vermont's control state structure is generally regarded by manufacturers as a positive component, though not without its share of hiccups and snags. According to most producers, the state does an excellent job supporting local production and the sales of products via state outlets, especially now that it has revamped internal communication between agencies and the central hub in Montpelier. As Vermont's spirits industry continues to rapidly grow and evolve, it appears that permitting, special events and enforcement may be the upcoming focus of attention.

Sivan Cotel, co-founder of Stonecutter Spirits and vice president of the DSCVT, sums up the collaborative nature of Vermont producers, legislators and enforcement:[48]

> *Seeing a successful industry that is thriving, maybe by accident, but doing well—legislators want to help add fuel to the fire. I think it is also attributable to our industry not being greedy. We limit ourselves to one or two things a year, nothing disagreeable, with the backing of the Division of Liquor Control. We don't get everything we ask for. Sometimes we ask for two and get one. Last year we asked for two and got zero. That's okay, we respect that. But we're going to show them—here are some of the pain points we are having in the industry. And here are a couple very minor changes to law. Most of the things we ask them to address are a sentence here and a sentence there. It's not asking to write a whole new this, that or whatever.*

He concludes:

> *The last part about this which is pretty new, there was never a lot of active alignment between the beer folks, the spirits folks, the wine folks and the cider folks. But this year we at the DSCVT asked the DLC to take a meeting with us, the beer folks, the wine folks and the cider folks. We had the first round table with all of us in the room together. It was specifically in response to something the DLC was thinking about that was going to affect all of us—let's get us all in the room together and help you understand the various things we all do before there are unintended consequences of the change you're thinking about. And can we help you make the change that you want to make but also make sure that it's focused.*

Chapter 6

DRAMATIS PERSONAE

We have a saying in Vermont: "If you don't like the weather, wait a minute." The same could be said for the Vermont spirits industry, an ever-changing environment full of new players and even newer products. More distillery startups enter the market every year, some founded by steadfast industry veterans while others are the dreams of impassioned hobbyists. The following section explores these dramatis personae, the characters and stories who breathe life into Vermont's rapidly expanding distillery scene.

I remain a firm believer that individuals should be allowed to showcase their own voices whenever possible. As such, the forthcoming profiles and vignettes heavily feature quotes from interviews with Vermont's numerous distillery owners, master blenders and head distillers. Their voices are those of this spirited movement.

APPALACHIAN GAP DISTILLERY

Lars Hubbard: *Founder/Owner/Chief Palate Officer*
Chuck Burkins: *Founder/Owner/Lab Mom/Quality Maven*

Vermont is frequently touted as a food and beverage Mecca. It's not difficult to find stretches of road or entire villages teeming with gastronomic delights, from the smallest cottage producers to the seemingly out-of-place national mega-brands. Middlebury's Exchange Street is one such corridor. Once a classic, bleak industrial park, it now brims with a host of thriving and inviting food and beverage enterprises.

Appalachian Gap Distillery, or "App Gap" as it's lovingly referred to throughout the state, is one of the several businesses that call the Exchange Street neighborhood home. Established in 2010, App Gap celebrated its fifth anniversary of operation on January 22, 2019. Despite having some rather heavyweight neighbors, founder Chuck Burkins notes that the environment in Middlebury has been a positive one.[49]

"The town understands us because they understand these guys. We were one of the first guys here. We broke ground as far as the waste guys understanding what we do. And we're on the same road here with not only Otter Creek Brewery and Woodchuck Cider, but Agri-Mark. So think about that in terms of [wastewater management]. Agri-Mark makes Woodchuck look small. So that makes everything a little more interesting. But yeah, I love it."

In addition to Agri-Mark, Woodchuck Cider and Otter Creek Brewery, Appalachian Gap Distillery shares the neighborhood with Stonecutter Spirits, Cabot Creamery, Aqua ViTea Kombucha and Vermont Coffee Company, among others.

There's a natural balance to the partnership found in Chuck and Lars, a balance that so beautifully imitates the art-science equilibrium inherent in distillation. Chuck explains the duo's origins and the founding of Appalachian Gap Distillery:

> *I'm a trained chemist. I have a degree in chemistry and worked as an analytical biochemist in the Boston area for fifteen or something years before I tossed it all to become a programmer. Lars used to be—at one point in his life, well, he used to be a lot of things—but he was a professional chef. So he's what I call the chief palate officer. He makes the decisions on flavors and things.*

With Chuck spearheading quality control and Lars on product development and flavor, the two operate as proverbial yin and yang, interconnected and complementary. This extends into their second business as well. Chuck continues:

> *Lars is an architectural specifier, which basically means he writes contract documents for big buildings and large construction projects. And I write*

software for architectural specifiers. My software is in use on five continents now, and he has specified some of the biggest buildings you've seen. I should say, big projects. Things like dorms (in a small way), hotels, casinos, one of the big buildings at the Smithsonian. That's one of our businesses. There's nothing wrong with specifications, but it's boring as hell. Distilling is not boring. That's why we got in the distillery business.

Lars adds:

The whole reason we did this was not because it's a great business but because we'd really wanted to do this and we think we can make it work as a business. But we have the luxury…I don't think luxury is the right word…it's a really expensive hobby.…Our main business is successful enough that we don't have to be paid by the distillery. So we are able to have all the money coming into the distillery to go back into the distillery. So at some point we'll be self-sustaining.

Many distilleries in Vermont run tight operations, and Appalachian Gap is no exception. Chuck elaborates on the company's structure:

Four people work here. I say "employees" [with a question mark] because I don't make any money on this place. My paycheck does not come from here. I was writing code when you arrived. We have a brand ambassador down in Brooklyn, but basically our sales staff here is Taylor and Chris in Vermont. And we have one guy in Boston.

Taylor and Chris also help in the day-to-day production, a grain-to-glass process that is as labor-intensive as it is rewarding. Chuck expands on App Gap's processes, providing insight into scale and order-of-operation:

So it starts there with the grain, we grind it up, and then it augurs into the mash and lauter tun. This is for a typical whiskey mash. Basically, this can take a half ton of grain, and there's a steel grate at the bottom there that essentially works as a false bottom. Then [the liquid] runs out into two fermenters. Our typical fermentation time is three to four days. Per fermenter, we're using about eight ounces of dry, active distiller's yeast, which has the advantage of being fairly neutral and fairly fast. You can feel this fermenter is warm to the touch. This one we've emptied out today and that's in the still right now. This one we'll empty tomorrow, and then tomorrow I'll be cleaning these two fermenters.

Appalachian Gap boasts an impressive commitment to sustainability. A solar array produces all of the distillery's electricity. Low-e coated, double-paned windows and efficient insulation help to regulate temperature. The distillery will be tapping into a new natural gas pipeline in order to run off renewable gas created from organic sources. Chuck notes that the distillery regularly tests its waste products in order to mitigate pollution risks and freely donates its spent grain to local farms.

"Less than one-tenth of 1 percent of our BOD-containing waste hits that trench drain. Basically, the only stuff that hits the trench drain has been hit with soap. Most of it goes out to farmers. They take the spent grain and the liquid and use them to feed cows."

Innovation is a fundamental element of Appalachian Gap's day-to-day operation. The distillery's whiskey still boasts a bespoke design, complete with hand-fabricated and purpose-built parts. Chuck explains:

> Our still was designed by Duncan Holaday and then put together here out of parts from California, New Jersey, some from Vermont and some things that were fabricated by a team he put together. It's a good whiskey still. Generally speaking, we'll run something around an 8 to 10 percent wash and come out about 25 to 35 percent low wines. We store up the low wines and run a second distillation.

Two additional stills produce vodka and gin, respectively. The smallest of the three stills, the dedicated gin still, is the company's former research and development still and can produce roughly a dozen twelve-bottle cases per day. The two larger stills can produce about four times that amount. Once produced, spirits are either conditioned before bottling or are sent to rest in App Gap's adjoining barrel house.

Chuck continues, "We don't refrigerate or heat our barrel warehouse, so [temperature] is all ambient. Which means during the winter, this gets cold. So when we do our barrel records, when we do our barrel inventory, we have the problem that the ink will freeze in the pens sometimes."[50]

Adirondack Barrel Cooperage supplies the barrels for the majority of Appalachian Gap's aged products, with some specialty port barrels making an occasional appearance. Whiskey, brandy and other fun surprises inhabit but a small portion of the large warehouse, a promise of future releases and proof of the distillery's dedication to the integrity of the maturation process.

We've passed the pilot stage more or less—there's nothing else we plan on piloting for the near future. We've got other things coming out, but those are already made. We don't have any special plans for anything. We plan on making bourbon. We don't plan on releasing anything soon. We don't have any in barrels yet. We only use thirty-gallon barrels if we can't get fifty-three-gallons, and we won't use anything under a thirty-gallon for a whiskey. I think, personally, to get a great whiskey—I think it helps to have a longer time with bigger barrels.

Appalachian Gap's current product line features a diverse array of both the traditional and the ingenious. Ridgeline, the distillery's flagship whiskey, is the easy-going lovechild of bourbon and Irish whiskey. Chuck describes the aging process: "It's aged in new bourbon barrels, used bourbon barrels and used port wine barrels for two or three years. They're aging parallel. Blended and then married in a port wine barrel between weeks and months. And we bottle from there."

"I find that bourbons are sometimes too sweet, too harsh, too acidic," continues Lars. "It's hard to find good bourbon. And Irish whiskeys are sometimes too dull. So why not find an in-between?"

Papilio, on the other hand, is something completely unique. An agave-maple spirit composed of 80 percent agave and 20 percent maple, the tequila-like spirit may ferment for over twenty days before being distilled twice. The aged version, Papilio Reposado, is then placed in an American oak barrel.

Lars explains, "Papilio was different. We were trying to come up with something completely unique that nobody else has even thought up. I have a weird brain that said, 'Maple tastes kind of smoky, agave tastes kind of smoky. Maybe together they'd make something?' Chuck thought I was out of my freaking mind."

In addition to Ridgeline and Papilio, App Gap produces Fractal and Snowfall, a vodka and unaged whiskey, respectively, each distilled from a grain bill of 45 percent barley, 30 percent corn and 25 percent rye; Kaffekask, a coffee-distilled white whiskey based on a Swedish drinking tradition; and their gins, Mythic and Peregrine. Mythic Gin, distilled with juniper, balsam fir and Szechuan peppercorns, among other botanicals, took Lars six months to develop. Peregrine, on the other hand, took only a few trials.

Lars delves into the origins of the two gins:

With Mythic, my wife challenged me to make something she'd like better than Hendricks. We were thinking we don't want to make a dry gin.

Everyone does it, and a lot of gins are dreadful. So we wanted to make a gin that is really full and round and textured....Peregrine only took me three batches because I'm getting better at it. I had three basic paths I could have gone down: the dry French wheat concept; I was thinking we could have done something like Bison Grass, a sort of flavored vodka from Russia; and then I was thinking, the spirit that comes off our still is so flavorful that going more towards the Genever end of things is what we originally thought. So I decided to go in the Dutch direction. Everything in there is kind of traditional Dutch except the weird amounts of cumin and orange.

In addition to these staples, the distillery also releases small batches of its Drumlin Rye whiskey, made from 100 percent rye grown within twenty-five miles of the distillery; Morning Sunshine, a whiskey distilled from Drop-In Brewing's Sunshine & Hoppiness Golden Ale; and Aqua Vodka, a collaborative product distilled using kombucha byproducts and made for Aqua ViTea Spirits.

"Our spirits are balanced, rich in flavor, utterly unique and MADE RIGHT HERE," declares Appalachian Gap's website. It's a declaration that the App Gap team undeniably and painstakingly champions from start to finish.

CALEDONIA SPIRITS

Ryan Christiansen: *President/Head Distiller*

Recognized throughout the United States for its dedication to a regional agricultural economy and for the distillery's widespread use of raw honey as a keystone ingredient, Caledonia Spirits is one of Vermont's most well-known spirits producers. Until recently, Caledonia's operation produced forty thousand cases annually out of its original 6,500-square-foot distillery in Hardwick, Vermont. In the summer of 2019, Caledonia Spirits moved into a brand-new 27,000-square-foot facility in Montpelier, Vermont.[51]

President Ryan Christiansen comments, "We're really focused on this whole facility, designed to take people from the grain in the silos through the production process, right to the cocktail lounge where we can actually teach people how to make a good, proper cocktail. That's a really important part of all this."

Customers enter into a tasting room and cocktail lounge, complete with a prominent thirty-two-foot bar made from Barre, Vermont granite. A long, wide corridor extends from the rear of the front-of-house space to a large viewing window that showcases the distillery's main nine-thousand-square-foot production floor.

> *This is the landing point of the tour. From this point you can look into the distillery, the lab, the bottling line. Some of the equipment has come down; Hardwick is still operational at this point. This is our Christian Carl five-hundred-gallon pot still. So we're going to have a five-plate whiskey column and two twenty-plate vodka columns. Basically takes that whole window. That's Route 2 over there, so the visibility is great.*

A bespoke building, the Caledonia Spirits team has ensured that production and future growth occurs as seamlessly as possible.

> *A production loop runs around the outside wall. Our GNS-based products run along the smaller loop on the inside. Everything lands in this area. From here it can go to barrels. This [adjacent room] will be our barrel room for now. It's designed so we can put another production loop in here and we can do offsite barreling if we need to.*

It's a massive step up from where Ryan began.

> *We started out with a little fifteen-gallon direct fire still. We produced about two cases of gin per distillation [with a] fire underneath the still that's producing 160-proof spirits. We'd run that once a week. Then eventually twice a week. Then five times a week. Then ten times a week. Then I was turning that thing on fifteen times a week. I'd come in at 4:00 a.m., leave at 9:00 p.m....So eventually we scaled up into a three-hundred-gallon still. One distillation on the three-hundred-gallon still was basically a week of production.*

Caledonia Spirits produces Barr Hill Gin, Tom Cat Gin and Barr Hill Vodka, each featuring the nuances of raw honey. Founded in 2009 by Todd Hardie, a lifelong beekeeper, the distillery was initially a means of diversification into additional value-added products.

Todd Hardie (*left*), founder of Caledonia Spirits, and Ryan Christiansen (*right*), current president of Caledonia Spirits. *Courtesy of Caledonia Spirits.*

Todd is a lifelong beekeeper who absolutely loves agriculture. He's invested his own time in agriculture. He was a beekeeper hobbyist turned into a commercial beekeeper and became a sort of pioneer of educating people in raw honey and the importance of pollinators in our food system. When I met Todd in 2011, he had recently sold his apiary. He owned a winery in Hardwick which was struggling, and he was hoping to solve the struggle of the winery by diversifying into spirits. He had an interest in getting into distilling, but Todd himself is a beekeeper. He's not a fermenter or distiller.

Enter Ryan Christiansen, fermentation enthusiast and owner of a local homebrewing store.

Around the same time, I was looking to open up a brewery. I owned a homebrew store in Plainfield and was contemplating expanding the homebrew store into a brewery and homebrew store all in one. I met Todd and was captivated by his love for agriculture. I realized that distillation is really just an agricultural opportunity. The amount of throughput you can put through a distilling facility is enormous, and the impact you can have on a small farmer is incredible.

While passionate about whiskey, Ryan quickly found that producing a farm-to-glass product using Vermont-grown grain wasn't as straightforward as it seemed.

I was coming from a beer-brewing background. I wanted to work with grains. Slowly, over time, I realized that there wasn't any local, organic grain-growing in the state. At that time—there is now, which is amazing. Back in 2011, Todd and I would go up and visit Jack Lazor. We had a very small distillery and a very small appetite for how many times we wanted to turn on our still—it wasn't very aggressive—and Jack would say, "Well, I can sell you all my whiskey grains, but then I wouldn't have anything to feed my cows." It was very eye-opening to me that a brand-new startup distillery was about to take all the grains from the guy who wrote the book about growing grains organically in the Northeast.

With that, Ryan and Todd turned their focus to gin and vodka.

We decided at that point that our largest agricultural impact would be with what we could do with the beekeepers and Barr Hill. It used to be about 650 pounds of honey per year. It's now about 60,000 to 90,000 pounds of honey per year. Think about the impact that we are having with one family of beekeepers. They're truly doing everything they could do to keep up with our needs, but in really a wonderful and harmonious way. They're not out to market selling and coming up with fancy packaging ideas. They're making sure that they don't have mites in the hives, and if they do get mites, they are nipping it in the bud right at the start. Their pesticide usage is incredibly low. If we need additional honey, they're able to vet all the other beekeepers based on the standards they've set.

As Ryan says, Barr Hill is a gin brand. A simple product of three ingredients, Barr Hill Gin is designed to let honey shine.

The gin is a GNS base. It goes through the botanical extraction stills. We're distilling with juniper. The raw honey is bringing the botanical complexity. Barr Hill is designed to be simple, sort of like the food movement right now. You can throw a hundred ingredients at something or you can come up with something simple and brilliant. The logic with Barr Hill is that there is so much complexity and depth with raw honey—let's figure out a way to showcase that. It's a canvas of juniper with the goal of outlining the complexity of honey. We think of bees as our botanical gatherers.

Gin isn't gin without juniper berries. *Courtesy of Caledonia Spirits.*

That said, honey is an extremely multifaceted product, and featuring honey in a spirit comes with its own set of difficulties.

There's so much mystery to what the bees actually do and what they're actually capable of, where they've been, etc. From a quality control aspect, it's beautifully challenging. We've set parameters that we understand how to manage within, but it's by all means a moving target. Seasonality, year to year, rain…bees need water just to keep the hive cool. What's going on with climate change—suddenly this creek dries up and the bees aren't going over here to collect pollen anymore. They're going over there to collect pollen. Well, there are apple blossoms over here and it's goldenrod over here. The honey is changing. Not because of apple blossoms and goldenrod, but because the creek dried up. So there are a lot of these things that are just completely out of our control.

In 2015, Todd stepped back from distilling, sales and marketing and returned to a life of farming.

Todd and I sat down to figure out what the long-term plan is here. How do we maybe bring in a partner so Todd could find an exit and so I could become a more serious partner? The resolution we came up with was that I bought the company, with a couple of partners, from Todd. Then Todd took the proceeds from selling the company and invested it in grain growing. So Todd's now farming about one hundred acres certified organic—rye, barley—basically remembering all the challenges we had of sourcing good quality raw materials and really putting his money where his mouth is and saying, "We can solve this."

Now, finally, Ryan can make his whiskey. "We've collaborated to come up with a new whiskey brand, which is not to market yet. But we're making it now. We made twelve barrels in the first year—from his land. We made twenty-four barrels the second year. We're going to make thirty-six barrels this year. Slowly, over time—this facility has been built to make a heck of a lot more."

Until Caledonia Spirits releases its anticipated whiskey, Barr Hill enthusiasts keen on an aged product can enjoy Tom Cat, its barrel-aged gin. A happy accident, the unique spirit was born of necessity and named after an icon of the British gin craze.

Ryan explains, "It took us nine months to scale up—took us nine months to re-create Barr Hill Gin from the fifteen-gallon still to the three-hundred-gallon still. So it didn't go as planned. We really thought it would be easy, but it wasn't easy at all."

While some test batches were outright scrapped, Ryan eventually saw an opportunity to keep batches—quality batches that otherwise missed the profile of the original.

> *I had already foolishly purchased a pallet of barrels. The barrels were there, upstairs, just drying out. I was like, "Man, this gin is going down the drain. Those barrels are going to develop leaks. They'll never seal." It was really just a means of procrastination of putting the gin down the drain, but I put the gin in the barrel. It was a brand-new oak barrel. It was a barrel that I thought I'd make bourbon with. It was just a few weeks in the barrel. We pulled a sample and thought, "This is really good. This is really something." We left it in the barrel, checked on it every month or so. After about four to six months, it had this bourbon-meets-gin thing going on.*

Ryan and the Caledonia team named it Tom Cat after the Old Tom–style gins that proliferated during the British gin craze.

> *The black cat represented someone who had Old Tom gin. If you were walking down the alley, you'd see a little black cat. [There was] probably a coin slot and tube in the wall. And for a penny, someone would pour a shot of really shitty gin out of the tube. So everybody in town, including the homeless and poor, were getting drunk on gin when gin was supposed to be banned. The reality was that there were people barricaded on the inside running these incredibly lucrative businesses. The black cat is a really cool story, so we started calling it Tom Cat.*[52]

Storytelling remains such an important part of the craft spirits industry. Distilleries throughout Vermont capitalize on images of idyllic green mountains, adventurous ski runs and the intentional, "slow" lifestyle inherent in Vermont culture. Employing nearly fifty individuals and distributing to at least thirty states and international markets, Caledonia Spirits is among the larger distilleries in the state, yet Ryan still recognizes the importance of maintaining a cohesive narrative.

"We're telling a honey story right now. We're telling a beekeeper's story."

DANGER CLOSE CRAFT DISTILLING

Steve Gagner: *Founder/Distiller*
Matt Kehaya: *Founder/Distiller*

"Veteran Owned. Veteran Distilled. Keep your friends close and your whiskey Danger Close." The website for Danger Close Craft Distilling is a landing page and nothing more—a handful of brief statements and a powerful logo, working together to invoke an air of secrecy and purpose. It leaves you wanting, needing, to know more.[53]

The new St. Albans–based distilling project, launched in a large garage by the team behind 14th Star Brewing Company, is one of the newest in Vermont. At the time of writing, it has yet to bottle product, though an inaugural release is right around the corner. Founders Steve Gagner, Matt Kehaya and Zac Fike all served together in the army—Steve and Matt together in Iraq and all three in the same battalion in Afghanistan—and supporting military veterans remains a core tenet of the distillery.

The brewery came first, a way for brothers-in-arms to continue spending quality time together. Steve explains:

> We deployed twice together. You develop a bond you're not going to develop in any other scenario. Especially going to Iraq and to Afghanistan at unique times together, we knew that we wanted to do something together in retirement once we got done. And we started planning from there. When we started, we were the twenty-third brewery in Vermont. Our plan was to go fairly slow. We started in a space not much bigger than this [garage]. We were doing it more as a way to get together, just spending time together on the weekend. It naturally grew quite fast to the point we were making our five-year plan in year two.

From 14th Star Brewing Company grew Danger Close Craft Distilling, a passion project. Steve continues:

> We've always had an interest in distilling since we've been brewers and knowing that process. Obviously, you can't distill without having a license. So we took it on as another hobby, and we included our other friend Zac, who runs Purple Hearts Reunited. He's joined us because he wanted to get more into the process. He's heavily involved with the brewery as well, and we took him on as a third person. We're working towards keeping it in the

same lines as we do with the brewery—the quality of the product, veteran-owned and run and support veteran programs within the community. We haven't released any product yet, and we all have other jobs as well. We're kind of doing this as a proof-of-concept first to see if it's something we can go bigger into like we did with the brewery. We're putting things in barrels, letting it age.

Matt adds, "The beauty of it is the symbiotic relationship. We don't have to create a brewery here to create a distiller's beer. We give our recipe to our team at 14th Star and they brew it for us, and we bring it here. That way we're not transferring alcohol, just selling sugar water to ourselves. That makes it very clean in terms of paperwork."

The grain-based sugar water—"wort" as it's known in the brewery world—arrives at Danger Close and is fermented into a distiller's wash. From there, the wash is run through the distillery's small, unique still. Steve explains:

This is a grundy from Commonwealth Brewing in Massachusetts. It was Paul Sayler's from Zero Gravity. When we were growing our brewery, he lent us four of these to increase our capacity. They're not great tanks for anything, but they're really good for a lot of things. When we didn't need them anymore, we gave them back to him. They're some of the first craft brewing tanks in America. We mentioned, "It would be really cool to make a still out of them." So he said, "Keep one, it's yours." So it's taken its next life. We welded some new feet to it, because they were literally rusting off.

It's a straightforward and intuitive still, a classic example of a self-modified piece of equipment—steadfast, no frills, purpose-driven.

It's an electric still. We run about ninety gallons max capacity, generally, and that's pushing it. When we're doing stripping runs, we'll have to back it down to keep it from [flooding] the column. It's really happy with seventy-five gallons. Ninety gallons is pushing it. We take the beer out of the totes, strip it. Low wines go here [in this tank]. We'll generally strip out the entire tote and get a decent amount of low wines and then do nothing but spirit runs, which go into this other grundy he gave us. Or they go to a barrel.

The barrels are produced by Green Mountain Grain & Barrel, another Vermont-based and veteran-owned business. Mac Broich, one of the founders of the cooperage, served in the same unit as Matt, who details further the relationship between Danger Close and the GMG&B team.

We've got their very first barrel, and that's the first barrel off their new CNC machine. We'd like to use them for all our wood as long as they can support us. We don't plan on using outside barrels unless they can't support us or we are getting special barrels for finishing. Those are whiskey barrels that were used for syrup, so when we made the maple spirit, we put it in those. But as far as bourbon goes, the plan is to just use Tony and Mac's barrels.

A steady supply of barrels will continue to be important for Danger Close, which plans to produce primarily bourbon and potentially some other aged spirits.

Steve outlines the plan:

Those bourbon barrels will become whiskey barrels. Eventually, probably, become rum barrels. Or beer barrels. Or brandy. Or syrup barrels, back to rum barrels, then down to the brewery. The number of uses will depend on what we can get out of the barrels. Initially, we are going to source some whiskey, but that's not really for in-state sales. That's for distribution to military installations, mostly to get the word out about the brand. And then the bourbon is mostly for in-state sales.

True to Vermont, Matt notes that the team also has a maple spirit in production. "We're dabbling. We have some maple spirit over there that is distilled pure maple syrup. We're doing some test runs on some maple bourbon barrels already."

As the Danger Close spirits near fruition, Steve, Matt and Zac will begin to incorporate elements of social, veteran-focused outreach into their operations. Matt expands on the concept:

For the distillery, we're looking more at hands-on work with veterans. Actually getting them small business experience and seeing how that process works. Talking them through how they can do it themselves. We realized that a lot of veterans don't translate what they get from the military over to the civilian world. And now, during this second business, we've determined that there are so many things that come naturally from being in the army or in the military service. Management roles, HR roles, safety roles, planning for future growth and things of that nature—it's all stuff we do. It's just taking it from a combat role to putting it into a corporation. So we really want to highlight that type of stuff here—enhancing that relationship with veterans and helping them to find something afterwards.

Steve continues:

A small business is really like being in a military unit. You have a mission. You motivate people towards that mission, navigating pitfalls. We're not teaching them necessarily how to be alcohol entrepreneurs, but we're using this as an example of marketing, production scheduling and human resources. If you can see it and touch it, even if it's for a different business, it's similar. The biggest thing is that we're not giving them the skills. The skills already exist. It's the process.

Danger Close Craft Distilling strives to produce quality spirits while simultaneously providing valuable services and support for Vermont's veteran community. The distillery's name is itself a strong symbol of its military roots and desire to do good work close to home. Steve says:

Danger Close is a military term for when you're calling artillery that is going to impact really close to your position. The enemy is really close on top of you. We want to help those veterans who are being told by corporate America, "You don't have what we're looking for." We really want to make an impact close to home. That's why we're doing this. It's not to make a million dollars. It's not to become the biggest distillery in Vermont. It's about making that impact. That's where Danger Close comes from.

Steve laughs, "And it's a pretty dope name."

Hell's Gate Distillery

Judi St. Hilaire: *Founder/Viticulture/Distiller*
Joe St. Hilaire: *Founder/Vermont Currant/Distiller*

Farm distilleries, those distilled spirits plants that produce spirits from products grown on their own farms, are hard to find. Both farming and distilling are incredibly time-consuming processes that require a multitude of diverse skills and inputs. Started in late 2016, Hell's Gate Distillery is one of a handful of farm distilleries in Vermont, a marriage of farm-grown grapes, hand-cultivated black currants and Vermont artisan spirits.[54]

Co-owners and siblings Joe and Judi St. Hilaire founded Hell's Gate Distillery at their family's farm in Georgia, Vermont, a few minutes south of St. Albans. The name "Hell's Gate," perhaps an odd choice at first glance, is firmly rooted in Georgia's history. Judi stumbled on the town's unique nickname while researching local history with her fourth-grade class. "During the War of 1812 era, there was a trade embargo on Canadian trade. The town upheld the embargo, which made it hard for smugglers to get through, so it became known as Hell's Gate—getting through Hell's gate."

Joe picks up the story: "Dad bought the farm in '87, I believe, and we had sheep here. It was an old dairy barn way back, with some cheese making. My dad bought it and built a house in the back. He raised sheep—hothouse lambs—and shipped everything to Canada. Eventually, it wasn't paying out. My sister purchased the barn and property; she has a house way back."

Judi continues:

> *I came here in '94 and I was teaching. My dad wasn't really doing a lot with the farm. We ended up buying it. My dad had started grapes. At the beginning, I was selling the grapes to Shelburne Vineyards. I was dabbling with that, seeing what I could do with grapes. The next year, we planted everything else. It got to a point where I thought, "Gosh, what am I going to do with all these grapes?" I started to quickly figure out that it wasn't a profitable venture to just sell grapes. We had to do our own thing with the grapes.*

Judi continues to manage the vineyard, and Joe focuses on the black currants. Together, the pair maintains about 2,000 currant bushes and about 1,200 grapevines, roughly four and a half and two and a half acres of plants, respectively. They also run Vermont Currant, a business that produces value-added products made from black currants.

It's a balanced partnership, as Joe remarks:

> *We harvest together. She'll tell you how to do the grapes. I do the currants. You tell me when we're ready to roll and I'll grab the people. I call my friends, we grab a shitload of people. The currants are the same way.*

Aerial photo of Hell's Gate Distillery and vineyard. *Courtesy of Hell's Gate Distillery.*

"They're ready next week," I say. "Let's go, we're ready to pick next week." We go crazy. We harvest. We built a cool room at the other end. We harvest up, then we crush and squeeze. We pipe everything through the building to our tanks.

The cool room has been a huge boon to production. "That's new this year. In the past, we'd harvest and then we'd really be up all night. It was hot out, so we'd have to get it harvested, crushed, pressed and into tanks. This year we built that little room, just an insulated room with an air conditioner. If we can't get to them right away, they at least stay cool until morning."

Joe and Judi not only use the juices of their currants and grapes, but they also use the byproducts of the pressing processes. After the currants are pressed for juice, the remaining solids become part of the Vermont Currant teas and meat rubs. The grape pomace, on the other hand, is reused to make grappa, a type of brandy commonly consumed in Europe as an after-dinner digestive spirit.

To learn more about the distilling industry, Joe and Judy enrolled in a Vermont Technical College distilling course taught by industry veteran Duncan Holaday.

Judy reminisces about the class: "There was another gentleman who already had his still. 'You really need a big still,' he said. We stuck to our

Family and friends help with the grape harvest at Hell's Gate Distillery. *Courtesy of Hell's Gate Distillery.*

guns, and we're really happy we did that. Although we probably spend a little extra time with the distilling, if we're only going to distill what we produce, we're not going to need a three-hundred-gallon still."

The bulk of Hell's Gate's production occurs in the fall, with Joe getting in early—around two or three o'clock in the morning—and Judi relieving him in the late morning or early afternoon. "It works well because we have different strengths. Different personalities," states Judi.

Joe agrees:

> *I'm on one end, she's on the other. We usually meet in the middle. For markets, her husband helps her. We swap off. She'll have a weekend, I'll have a weekend, so we get some time. My wife comes with me to the markets and helps. When we're in a pickle, we'll go after them first and they'll help, you know. But it's me and her. The only other people that come on are for harvest.*

Farmers' markets provide the bulk of Joe and Judi's sales. A small tasting room, complete with a bar crafted from farm-harvested wood, allows for sales opportunities direct from the distillery. The distillery's distinct line of farm-to-glass products appeals to a wide variety of consumers, and while they are not yet distributed to Vermont state stores, Judi and Joe say their products will soon be available to restaurants.

Grape-derived brandies are not as well known in the United States as some other spirit varieties, but Judy masterfully navigates the descriptions and tasting notes of the Hell's Gate product line.

> *We started out with the Regal Onyx, the 65-proof flavored brandy. This doesn't have as much currant flavor as the liqueur, but it has more of an alcohol-forward finish. The 40-proof Black Pearl is our liqueur. Both of these are the black currant products we started out with. The next thing we came out with is the grappa.[55] The grappa is 90-proof and came out in April 2018. It's from our Marquette grapes. The 1812 came out in October 2018 and is made with Frontenac Gris grapes, distilled. It's put in the tank with maple chips we'll cut in the spring, so there's a lot of sap. They're put in a forge and charred, and the spirit sits in a tank with them. This will be the first time, this year, that we've started to market the Regal Onyx and the 1812 in a smaller bottle.*

The St. Hilaires' attention to detail is indicative of producers who truly engage their product from start to finish—from seedling to still and beyond. Citing their French heritage, Judi remarks that they are no strangers to small-batch production. "We grew up in a winemaking family. My father's made wine since we were kids. He did everything. He used grapes, even dandelions."

When you stop by, be sure to ask Judi about those dandelions. She has a great story.

Hooker Mountain Farm Distillery

Carrie Randolph: *Founder/Farmer*
Kempton Randolph: *Founder/Farmer/Distiller*

Unless it is a museum piece, no distillery operates as if it were the 1800s. Technology has come so far in such a short amount of time. While the nuts and bolts of distilling remain the same—the basic concepts of evaporation, condensation and concentration have not changed since the advent of distilling—the processes have been refined several times over, and equipment is considerably more efficient. Some folks find, however, that there are lessons to be learned from our past. As Walt Whitman once said in the preface of his 1855 *Leaves of Grass*, "Nothing is better than simplicity."

Enter Hooker Mountain Farm Distillery, contemporary Vermont's first diversified agricultural distillery. Its story is one of traditionally inspired farm distilling—a story of from-the-land, back-to-the-land, do-it-yourself production. For Carrie and Kempton Randolph, it's what works. It's what makes sense.[56]

The seed for a distillery was planted in Kempton's mind while reading a book on the history of New England farming.

> *We have a distilling history here in the state that a lot of people are disconnected from because it was so long ago. In Cabot—this was the thing that first planted the idea of a distillery—I had been reading an agricultural history book about New England that happened to mention Cabot and Peacham. Cabot had, in 1812, a dozen distilleries just in this town. Peacham had twenty-something. This region was known for its whiskey. It would get shipped down to Boston and up to Montreal. A lot was smuggled over the border. There was an embargo at the time. There were embargos with the sugar production and a lot of the Caribbean colonies. England was upset with us. The trade was interrupted. It allowed for this distilling industry to prosper up here, and it was all ag-based. It was mostly centered around potatoes.*

As they dug into the idea more, Kempton and Carrie realized that their farm-distillery model had unintentionally evolved to mimic the farm's mid-nineteenth-century iteration. History had, to a degree, ventured to repeat itself. Kempton noted the parallels:

> *The harvesting and processing [of grain] is really labor intensive. Potatoes would grow really well in this soil. And we had all the Scotch and Irish immigrants, and they were the ones who knew how to distill, and they knew potatoes. We have the agricultural census records from the farm in the 1800s, and we basically run the same farm they had here in 1860, without even trying [to do so]. They grew about the same amount of oats. They grew corn. They grew potatoes, and they had four milk cows. They did butter. They hayed. For their grain, when I ran the numbers, I was like, "Oh…they grew a little bit more than we do."*

The farm was first a sheep farm and then a dairy farm. It then diversified a bit while retaining a small dairy operation. The farm closed around 1950–55 and was reborn with Kempton and Carrie as Hooker Mountain Farm, a value-added, diversified farm-distilling operation. Kempton describes the Hooker Mountain operation:

> *We grow an acre of corn—in a good year, two or three thousand pounds of corn. I grow about five acres of grain total. The corn is the most labor intensive, so that's why it's only an acre. I do mostly oats, a little bit of barley, and I grow potatoes.... We milk four cows and just got a few more. This summer it will be up to six. We do some pigs. All our distilling spent grain we feed out to our pigs.*

Diversification versus specialization is a constant debate for small farms. Kempton and Carrie find that a diversified operation meshes well with the inherent flexibility encouraged by distillation.

Kempton continues:

> *The distillery is such a unique business in that it can take in almost any input we produce. It allows us to farm in a way that was common 120 years ago: the small, really diversified farm. Nobody really does it anymore. You can't make a living growing four or five acres of grain and milking five or six cows—but you can if you're running a distillery.*

Carrie adds:

> *It is really awesome for small farmers, even if you're not going to be farming yourself but are collaborating with these small-scale growers. When we run the numbers for what we'd get if we sold our grain or sold our milk, we can't make it work. But you put it into something value-added like spirits, and all the sudden it's a whole different game. You've got products which are interesting, high-quality and which people are excited about and want to drink and experiment with. And also, they feel good about it. It is a good product. There are no artificial flavorings or color. People are more aware of that stuff now, even in alcohol, than they ever have been before. I think there's room if you're a distiller to seek out small grain-growers and pay them a decent wage for their grain. Because you know that you're going to use it in a way that is going to earn a lot more money than just feeding cows, you know?*

Hooker Mountain's distillery is small, built by hand from wood grown on the farm. The wooden structure melds seamlessly with its picturesque agricultural setting. Everything is produced on a small eighty-gallon still,

Kempton and Carrie built the distillery from farm-grown wood. *Courtesy of Hooker Mountain Farm Distillery.*

using open-topped cypress tanks for fermentation and a variety of woods, also farm-harvested, for aging. A wood-fired masonry heater and wood-fired three-hundred-gallon pot still are currently used to heat water, though Kempton hopes to use the latter for stripping runs in the near future. Everything considered, Kempton notes that it's a huge step up from the single thirteen-gallon still he started with.

We have a line of maple sodas that we do with our own syrup, and I was making the flavorings using steam distillation—steaming yellow birch bark and spruce tips for the essential oils and using them to flavor the sodas. That's how I got into distilling was through the essential oils and steam distillation. And then I was like, this actually would be really great if we were making alcohol. And then I started building the distillery. It's been interesting. I didn't study with anybody. I taught myself how to do all this, how to set it all up.

In case you haven't figured it out by now, diversification is a core theme at Hooker Mountain Farm. Not only do Carrie and Kempton run a diversified farm, but they also produce over twenty different spirits in small batches throughout the year. Eight or so products are made year-round, while the rest are seasonal offerings. Farm-grown grain and potatoes play a central role in Hooker Mountain's spirits production, as do the dairy cows.

Carrie delves into the integration of the dairy and distillery:

> *We milk twice a day. So we bring them* [to the milk parlor] *and hook up two at a time, and we have a small bucket milker. We have a little creamery and a little finished commercial kitchen. We separate out the cream—we do Woke, which is a milk-and-coffee bottled cocktail. That's made with our skim milk. And we do a chocolate milk version, basically. It's 20 percent alcohol.*

Kempton mentions that he and Carrie also utilize their whey byproduct.

> *Whey Good is about 50 percent whey in the finished volume. It's all from our cows. It's the same process you'd go through making cheese, when you separate the curds and are left with the whey. We got the idea from milk punch cocktails and thought we'd try it in a finished spirit. And it works great; people love it. It's creamy like milk, but it has almost a malted flavor to it.*

Six Hooker Mountain products are currently available through Vermont's Division of Liquor Control. Kempton goes through the list:

> *We distribute our Spruce gin, the Woke milk-and-coffee, the spirited cider (it's like a pommeau, a sweet cider and light rum) and then a Fernet[57] with hawthorn fruit and hops we grow here. We started another brand—our Poor Farm brand—which are spirits we just rectify. We have a vodka under that label, and we do a rum we age on sugar maple wood with a touch of maple syrup. We did those because we realized there was a price gap in the Vermont market with what was being offered. The rum is $23.99 and the vodka is $21.99. So we ran the numbers and could make it work, and it fills a price hole on the shelf.*

Rectifying may seem out of place for a farm distillery, but Carrie explains that the decision was a practical one that support their more creative endeavors. The decision to bottle a vodka and rum also supports their tasting room and cocktail bar, located at the Marshfield general store, just down the road from the farm. Carrie continues:

> You need to have vodka and rum if you're running a cocktail bar. So why not make them ourselves? That was our motivation, and then we said, "Well, people like this. Why not let it carry some more of the more labor-intensive products?" It's kind of hard for us though, because we started out as super purists. That's still our underlying philosophy, but we realize that there's a business side to this too. And some of it is a numbers game. You have to sell so much of something in order to support the products that you love which aren't necessarily going to sell the same way that vodka is going to sell. People love vodka. They know what it is, how to use it.

Hooker Mountain's whiskey offerings are varied and seasonal. Several may feature the farm's oats, while another highlights the farm's potatoes for a spirit reminiscent of Irish poitín.[58] Kempton also produces several unique

Spruce is but one of Hooker Mountain's unique spirits. *Courtesy of Hooker Mountain Farm Distillery.*

liqueurs. Birch is a grain spirit blended with yellow birch essential oils and aged on yellow birch wood, resulting in the refreshing wintergreen flavor characteristic of birch wood. The culturally inspired Génépy and Anisette, two herbal liqueurs, are also produced from time to time. Available primarily at farmers' markets, Hooker Mountain's spirits are frequently offered in small-format bottles meant to encourage customers to sample and collect different flavors. Patrons have come to expect unique, quality products.

According to Carrie, distilling is a natural part of the evolution of value-added farm products. "I think, as farmers, we have a natural inclination to make products that taste good, you know, and are a valuable product. In general, farmers take a lot of pride in having good meat, good eggs and good veggies. Distilling is a natural progression."

It may not always be the easiest agricultural outlet, but Carrie emphasizes collaboration and the importance of knowing and understanding personal goals. For Hooker Mountain, the distillery supports the farm.

We get asked by a lot of people: "From a cost standpoint, isn't it easier to purchase milk or whey?" "Absolutely. But for us, it's kind of flip-flopped. Our primary objective is to be farming, and the distillery is kind of the, "Oh my goodness, this would actually support a working small-scale farm!" Whereas if you really just want to be distilling, which is a perfectly admirable goal, then you don't necessarily need to run a farm. If you don't love it, it's really a huge commitment and a lot of time. So we try to tell people that you don't have to do both—you can collaborate.

"A rising tide lifts all boats" is a phrase I frequently hear when discussing Vermont's distilling industry. At the end of the day, it's always about intentionality, quality and, in many cases, Vermont's countless small farms.

Carrie stresses collaboration once more. "Vermont is really still all about agriculture. It's how we brand ourselves. This is a great way to support that."

Mad River Distillers

Alex Hilton: *General Manager/Chief Distiller*

Cottage industry is alive and well in Vermont, and in some cases, local governments have allowed owners to build and operate distilleries in secluded barns and outbuildings. Built in the mid-1800s, Cold Spring Farm is one such property. It was converted into a horse farm in the mid-1900s, and contractor-turned-distiller Alex Hilton renovated the rundown horse barn into a state-of-the-art distillery in 2011.[59]

I knew John Neegan and Maura Connely, the founders. I was a caretaker for them. I lived in this area and was working as a contractor building houses. They approached me for this project, and basically, that's how I came into the mix. I did all the construction work and renovations for almost two years. Over time, I became interested in what they were doing. They asked me towards the end of the construction phase if I'd be interested in staying on and running the operations here. We didn't really have any hands-on experience, so we just learned and taught ourselves as we went. We started with rum and corn whiskey and graduated on to bourbon and rye and all the different things we do now.

Alex and the team at Mad River Distillers produce on a 250-liter (about 66 gallons) Mueller pot still. A German-made workhorse, it handles all of the company's finish runs.

It's made in Stuttgart, and it's awesome. We love it. We just outgrew it a little bit. We still run all of our spirits through here, but about a year and a half to two years ago we bought a second still. This is an American still. We run it as a stripping still—it's a five-hundred-gallon pot still. You could in theory do finishing runs on it. We don't. We never intended to. It seemed like we'd get it and use it as a stripping still. Maybe someday we can finish on it, but I don't know we ever will.

Changing finishing stills is a big deal, requiring the balancing and tweaking of recipes and production processes to ensure that the quality and flavors of finished products are not compromised.

Our mash tun is a one-to-one ratio, a five-hundred-gallon batch size. And then we finish it over here [on the Mueller]. We were worried that if we started finishing on a different still it would change the profile and change the spirits. And it probably would. So it worked out pretty well that we can finish everything through here. We're running seven days a week and we have been for two or three years, trying to make as much as we can. We're pretty much at max capacity in this facility. So we're

Mad River's still is a classic example of German manufacturing. *Courtesy of Mad River Distillers.*

> *trying to build up inventory. We have some warehouse space down in Waitsfield that we use for storage.*

Because of its location on a residential property, the distillery's footprint is relatively constrained. The Waitsfield warehouse space is a valuable addition that allows for easier deliveries of ingredients and more bonded storage.

> *It's easier for us to get deliveries, glass, grain, all that stuff in bulk down there, and then we can bring it up here as need be. We're in the process of bonding that space, too, so we can transfer stuff in bond down there and bottle down there. Barrel storage is the hardest part for us. We don't want to build anymore here at the distillery. It doesn't make sense. But finding a spot that is zoned properly, that is close by, that has forklift or truck access—it's really tough. It's funny. When we started building this—for the first year anyway—we thought this was plenty of space and we were all good, but it's crazy how fast you fill it.*

Mad River Distillers manufactures its products from start to finish at the distillery, using local and regional ingredients whenever possible. "We're still doing the same core products from day one, pretty much. Everything is

Packaging and bottling are hands-on processes. *Courtesy of Mad River Distillers.*

grain to glass. We buy all our grains as locally or regionally as possible. You can't get everything locally or regionally, but we're doing our best."

Specializing primarily in aged spirits, Alex supervises the production of rums, whiskeys and brandy. All of Mad River's rums are made using the same base rum. From there, different methods of production help to differentiate the sugar-based spirits.

"We use demerara sugar as the base. We have our First Run Rum and then our Maple Cask Rum, which we age first in new barrels and then in maple syrup casks. We also have a Vanilla Rum, which is the only product we make that doesn't spend any time in a barrel. It's just infused with vanilla beans."

A fourth rum, PX Rum, is finished in Pedro Ximenez sherry barrels and won Double Gold for Best Aged Rum in the 2017 San Francisco International Spirits Competition. It's available in limited quantities at Mad River Distillers' satellite tasting room in Burlington, Vermont.

While Mad River's rums continue to bring home accolades and awards, America's palate remains enamored by whiskey.

The bourbon is our number-one [selling spirit] *for sure. Getting as much age on it as possible is the challenge. After that, I think it's probably the maple rum. But I think the rye is gaining on it. The rye is actually gaining a lot of traction across the board. It may be posing a threat to bourbon, too. I like the rye a lot, myself. We use a roasted chocolate malt. I always describe it to people like a coffee bean, kind of. We don't use much of it. A little bit goes a long way.*

In addition to its four-grain bourbon and 100 percent rye whiskey, the distillery engages in a series of collaborations with Vermont craft breweries. The results have yielded exciting and diverse results.

We started the Hop Scotch series. It's kind of like single malt. We've done it with Lawson's, Zero Gravity, 14th Star, Upper Pass, Otter Creek, von Trapp—a number of breweries. We still have some in the pipeline. We're trying to do some every year. We'll buy wort from them—different varieties and styles. Ferment it and distill it here. Age it for a couple years, ideally, and then release it as a kind of single malt whiskey. Which it is, but there are inevitably hops in it. It's a cool project. People are really interested in it. It's interesting how the different styles of beer come through in it.

Last but not least, Mad River Distillers makes brandy, a passion project of sorts that is largely inspired by Maura and John's love of Calvados, an apple brandy native to the Normandy region of France. "John and Maura wanted to do apple brandy. John loves Calvados. That was kind of where his idea came from for the distillery. And then he realized pretty quickly that, yeah, we could make apple brandy, but there are so many things we should make and could make."

Not everything goes according to plan, however. Running a distillery often means having to be flexible, rolling with punches and making the best of all situations.

We have our apple brandy, which is now called Mad Apple. It was originally called Malvados. But we had to change the name because it was too close to Calvados. The Calvados Commission of France asked us to change it, so we obliged. We got a letter from France and they were like, "Yeah, that's not going to work for us." But it was interesting because we had been selling it as Malvados for about three years before that happened. So I think that possibly we got enough traction, and initially they had no idea we were doing it. We changed it to Mad Apple last year in 2018.

"Think Globally, Distill Locally" is Mad River Distillers' catchphrase, a slogan that speaks not only of its commitments to using local grain, fresh spring water and fair-trade certified, sustainable sugar, but also of the inspiration of Calvados and New England's rum-laden past. A passionate hobby turned successful business, Mad River's story is one that resonates with so many of Vermont's small businesses.

This property, it was a horse farm. It has a number of old apple trees all over the property. That's what got John and Maura thinking apples and apple brandy. They wanted to do something cool with the property, get things up and running again. When you're using something, it tends to get taken care of better. Rather than letting this barn just fall down and go to shit, I think that was part of it too. It was initially meant to be a hobby, hence the smaller still. We didn't have a super clear plan as to where we were going, and then it grew. It was a lot of trial and error, a lot of screwing things up and figuring it out. We were way smaller as far as how much we were producing when we got started. But we've grown a lot in a relatively short amount of time, and the quality has improved tremendously.

OLD ROUTE TWO SPIRITS

Ryan Dumperth: *Founder*
Adam Overbay: *Founder*

Patience, research and development are some of the best words one can use to describe Old Route Two Spirits, one of Vermont's newest distilling operations. Incorporated in 2016 and fully licensed in 2017, the distillery already produces an impressive portfolio of rum, gin and specialty spirits, with whiskey on the horizon. While a young outfit, the team at Old Route Two pays special attention to the maturation process, using innovations in coopering and wood selection to craft a collection of uniquely aged products.

New distilleries occasionally have enough luck and capital to move into a truly bespoke building. More often than not, the majority of startups (especially in Vermont) repurpose used or vacant industrial or agricultural buildings. For Old Route Two, it was an explosive affair.[60] Founder Ryan Dumperth explains:

Maine Drilling and Blasting had this before us. It was really nice—well, sort of nice—to have them before here. Being a distillery, they had a room dedicated to explosives. So we put all of our boiler equipment and everything in there. All the fire would stay in one place, all the spirits in another place and there's a blast-proof wall in between. The not-so-nice thing was that when we first walked in here it smelled like the inside of a diesel tank. Because this was their maintenance bay—so we had to completely overhaul it. We had to put in drywall and new flooring down, but it shaped up nicely.

Once officially licensed, Adam Overbay and Ryan Dumperth started the experimental process of product development. Ryan continues:

We got licensed February 2017, started major research and development in March. The rum was the first thing we did. It took us about two and a half months to get our rum recipe. We tried a number of yeasts, a number of different molasses and sugars and things like that. We settled on LuWest out of Louisiana; they do blackstrap and turbinado [sugar]. They send us three-thousand-pound totes of blackstrap and one-ton bags of sugar, and we repurpose them after. We skew a little towards the molasses, but it's almost a fifty-fifty blend.

While happy with the results of the unaged white rum, Ryan and Adam ultimately concluded that competing against rum giants such as Bacardi was an unnecessary uphill battle. They then decided to pivot, instead using rum as a unique base spirit for gin. Ryan expands on the idea:

We made a really nice white rum. But trying to market white rum, you're competing against Bacardi. They can always have a thirteen-dollar bottle, and what are you going to do about that? So we took a look at it and said, "What if we use this as a gin base? What if we take this white rum, add juniper to it and some other botanicals?"

Gin is most frequently made with mass-produced neutral grain spirits but can be built from any base spirit so long as it is distilled with juniper berries during subsequent gin runs. Many craft distilleries use their own vodka as the base spirit for gin or develop other flavorful, unaged spirits such as brandy, rum or whiskey for a more distinct foundation.

So we went to Railyard Apothecary over in Burlington. Basically, we showed up and they thought we were crazy. We said, "We want two ounces of everything." We raided their shelves and had them tell us which herbs were local. We came back here and spent three weeks opening bags of herbs, smelling them and sorting them and figuring out what we thought would work and what wouldn't. That got it down to about thirty herbs. Then we started doing micro-distillations of single herbs, just to see. "Well, it smells like this but once you distill it what happens?"

Research and development is an arduous process. With its high botanical content and countless potential flavor combinations, gin development is often touted as the alchemy of the distilling world. Adam concludes the gin discussion, "You just have to play around, mix and match. Basically, we found, in the end, ten botanicals. We weighted ones we liked based on how likely we would be to find someone to grow them locally. We have ten botanicals, seven of which are grown either in the back woods of Morrisville or down at Free Verse Farm in Chelsea."

A dedication to using Vermont-sourced products is one of Old Route Two's driving principles. Ryan describes the team's approach to distilling, a tried-and-true combination of Vermont practicality and innovation:

We had a few goals: use as much Vermont stuff as possible, but not tie our hands back by using only Vermont product. No one is growing commercial juniper here, so that would never come from Vermont. It's our best effort to use what's here. It's a marketing thing and a way to support the ecosystem here in Vermont. There are so many great growers of really high-quality products, and we want to transform those into value-added products. For the gin, the great thing about the gin's recipe, is that we wanted it to be a taste of Vermont. That was an explicit goal. We want everything we do to be sippable. So in R&D, that was part of it. We want to bring in raw ingredients and do everything ourselves. Raw ingredients come in. Bottles come in. We fill and label in the back. We ship finished pallets. Everything is done here.

Ryan continues:

Another thing we wanted to do with our products was to try and bring something new to the category without being gimmicky. The gin, we designed it to be a sipping gin. There are very few gins you actually want to sip. We spent three months developing that recipe where Adam iterated with the samples first, just pouring them individually and building up the

Old Route Two Spirits features a modular production space and unique, multi-wood barrels. *Courtesy of Old Route Two Spirits.*

ten layers we ended up having. Then distilling and making sure it worked that way. The botanicals we use are really magical in the way that there's no one dominant flavor; they all harmonize nicely.

Adam adds:

That's kind of what I went for. In the gin, there's juniper of course. There's also lemon peel, lemon balm and lemongrass. Lemon peel obviously you can't grow here, but we get balm and grass. The chamomile has hints of pineapple that it throws in there. Then the wildcard in the gin is the spilanthes. It was one that originally might give it another citrus kick, but when you distill it loses all flavor but retains a little Szechuan peppercorn property where it makes your mouth water just a little bit at the back when the sip is done. We're very careful how we dose the gin with the spilanthes, but we think it gives it just a little something at the back.

In addition to the gin, Adam and Ryan produce a handful of aged rums. Adam explains:

With the rum, the difference is that we're using custom barrels. The woods are all hand-selected by US Barrel in Plattsburgh. The staves are all oak, and then we are using cherry, maple, ash and oak heads. So we're getting a lot of complexity at a young age. They're virgin barrels, and we're pulling on all those different types of woods that, I'm sure somebody's done it, but we haven't been able to find anybody. It's a nice twist, a consistent twist, and it adds a lot.

As with gin research and development, barrel aging requires a lot of time and patience. While you may have an idea of what will happen to a spirit, results frequently vary. This is especially true when trailblazing a path with woods other than white oak.

He continues:

Initially, the concept of those four woods was that we were going to marry them all together and have a single rum. And for the first six months, that worked for our blending experiments. Originally, we thought we were going to take it out, blend and bottle after six months. But the trajectory of improvement of flavor was so good each month over month. So we decided at one year we'll try it again, and that was the right call. It became a lot rounder and more sophisticated over a year. And we'll keep going, but it will be a year minimum for now.

The results of their maturation experiments yielded two distinct rums in what is now known as Old Route Two's Barrelhead Rum line: Cherrywood and Maple & Ash. The flavors produced by the cherrywood barrelheads, spicy like a rye whiskey, simply did not play well with the more subtle notes of maple and ash.

"The flavor just collapses and the spark goes out," says Ryan. It's really weird. It's not that it clashes, but when you take [the cherrywood] out, everything is great. We started doing the other permutations and found that the maple and ash really complement each other well. So, I guess we have two rums."

Old Route Two Spirits also makes Coffee Rum, a rum proofed down with Vermont Artisan cold brew coffee and barrel-aged for a year, and Viking Funeral, a spirit distilled from mead. Ryan describes the unique development of Viking Funeral:

So once we got that done, that became our full lineup: the gin, the two rums and the coffee rum. We started selling in mid-November and hit store shelves in December. And then [Viking Funeral] started as a limited run. Groennfell Meadery over in Colchester—Ricky the meadmaker there, he and I were chatting at a trade show. And I said, "I wonder what it's like to distill mead…" And he said, "I've wondered that too. I have the perfect mead for you." So they gave us three pallets of this mead because their bottling machine misfilled the bottles. So we took them, basically five thousand bottles, dumped them in the still and distilled it. That's the best way we've been able to describe it. And it sucks because in the U.S. this isn't a category; in Austria it would be schnapps. In Germany it would be schapps. In Denmark it would be aquavit. It's basically a honey aquavit or schnapps. It's warm, but it retained the honeycomb flavor. It's like fresh honeycomb. It's got a slight beeswax element to it and a bold, bold honey flavor behind it.

All of Old Route Two's spirits are developed on a ten-gallon Trident still and, after scaling up, are produced on a three-hundred-gallon hybrid pot still of the same make.[61] Adam shows off the distillery's lab and test environment, commenting on the equipment:

The test still has been a lifesaver. The lab's either inspection-ready or work-ready at all times. It's really been a lifesaver. It is the exact same still, just basically one-twentieth of the size. Pot still. Dephlegmator. Condenser. That's really it. Trident Stills are out of Maine. They did our whole kit: the still, the mash tun, our fermenters. They've all worked really well. We went with a modular design with [the fermenters]. Conceptually, I like conicals a lot for fermenting. But once they're in place, they're not going anywhere. When we ordered everything, we didn't know where we were going to be, what the space would look like. All our fermenters are designed so our forklift can pick them up, move them and put them down.

Subtle tweaks to the still allow Adam to guide the distillation, preserving or subduing flavors based on the end goal of the spirit. He continues his description of Old Route Two's distillation processes:

With the rum, we tend to run the still dephlegmator off and run it as a normal pot still. With the gin, we'll run it with the dephlegmator on and clean it up [the spirit] bit. The way I describe it, it's like adding artificial height to the column. That's all the dephlegmator does; it chills. It's a packed column—copper mesh. The interior is stainless, the copper on the outside is an exterior finish. I think that's worked out pretty well having the copper mesh as a sacrificial in there. It means I don't have to go climbing into stills to polish copper and clean them. When the mesh is done it's done, and we put new mesh in there. That's it.

"Necessity is the mother of invention," or so people say. In looking at Old Route Two Spirits, one might disagree. There is nothing "necessary" about using multiple woods as barrelheads or deciding to use a white rum as the base for Joe's Pond Gin. In many cases, innovation is as much about intentionality, observation and sweating the small stuff as it is adapting to the moment. Look closely at Old Route Two's bottles. From the regional maps with Route Two highlighted in red, to the alcohol-by-volume and proof of the spirits, it's all deliberate and calculated. It's all about producing the best spirits and presenting them in the best manner possible.

Ryan remarks:

It's 40.1 percent ABV—80.2 proof. I was driving south on I-89 and happened to notice the mile markers ticking down, and there's not a post there. I thought, "Well, they probably don't do that because people kept stealing it." And then, "Wait a minute, that's a valid proof." And now everything is 802-proof. We've tried everything at higher proofs; we're not specifically shooting for 80, but if it works at 80....When the rum was younger it was better at a higher proof.

SAXTONS RIVER DISTILLERY

Christian Stromberg: *Founder/Head Distiller*

"It was an interest, there was history, and I had an idea."

These three statements have likely inspired more start-up businesses than any others. In the early days of the craft distilling industry, especially here in Vermont, distillery owners were self-taught. In the late 1990s and early 2000s, there were no Vermont Technical College distilling courses, no Siebel Institute classes on distilling operations and technology and no craft distilleries offering weekend workshops. Distiller-owners had to capitalize on do-it-yourself spirit.

When Christian Stromberg founded Saxtons River Distillery in 2006, he built it all—concept, distillery, still—from the ground up.[62]

My training is engineering. I wanted my own business, and this idea had been floating in my head. I got fired from my last real job and decided it was time to do it. I had differences of how I thought things should be done, and ultimately, I always needed to have my own business. That's always been my mentality. I wanted the place to work like I thought it should versus just being an employee, shutting up and doing your job. So I said let's try this. I talked to my wife about it. I had built this barn for my wood shop. It's actually two stories, located on the Saxtons River, and thus the name of the distillery.

With a location secured and an idea in mind, Christian looked toward his family's history for further inspiration.

My great-grandmother was a moonshiner. My grandfather told me how to make what they'd made. When he was living with us at the end of his life, he'd seen me building a still. I'd built one when I was in college. And he told me roughly what they made and how, which we've re-created now. But it was a prohibition recipe, which was primarily "make it and don't get caught." Was it aged and perfected? Damn, that stuff was still warm when people drank it! It was about not getting caught. They did it to survive, and that's it.

We made…traditionally it's called krupnikas. It's Lithuanian. Poles call it krupnik. It's a honey-spiced liquor. And they're around; other people are making them now. But at the time, I didn't think there was much of a market for honey. And then Tennessee Honey came out and I thought, "Well, I guess I was wrong."

Not all was lost, however. The trials and errors of krupnikas eventually yielded Christian's first big hit, Sapling Maple Liqueur. Found on nearly every bar in Vermont, it's become a symbol of the Vermont spirits industry.

The maple industry is a tough one, requiring a large amount of labor and capital, and Vermont's workforce isn't getting any younger. Many Vermont-made spirits utilize the flavors and cultural cache of Vermont's maple industry, and distillers frequently work directly with local and regional sugaring operations to secure syrup in mutually beneficial arrangements.

The guys I deal with are old school, wood-fire guys. They still have tech; they use a vacuum. It's the reality of it. You're talking a massive difference in quantity—horizontal runs as opposed to gravity feed, etc. I wonder,

Saxtons River Distillery's portfolio heavily features maple syrup as an ingredient. *Courtesy of Saxtons River Distillery.*

though, because these guys aren't young. In general, I run into a lot of old people when I go to the events. It's an old industry. I hope some younger people get into it. There's money, but there's also a lot of investment. All I see is people slowly trying to find someone to take over their sugarbush because they can't afford it. The price is down, and it probably isn't ever going to be what it was, just because production has spiked everywhere else.

In addition to Sapling Maple Liqueur, Saxtons River produces Sapling Maple Bourbon and Sapling Maple Rye. Perc, a lightly sweetened coffee liqueur produced using cold-brewed Arabica coffee beans, is a great substitute for Kahlua. Finally, they have Snowdrop Gin. An American dry gin with eighteen botanicals (among them are juniper, ginger, cardamom, coriander, orange zest and star anise), Snowdrop Gin joins a long list of Vermont-made gins suitable for both classic cocktails and the ubiquitous gin and tonic.

All spirits produced by Saxtons River Distillery are distilled under vacuum, a rare method in an industry dominated by steam-powered and electric stills.

We distill under vacuum. There aren't many of us. There are certain things that are fantastic about it, but it's hard. Other than changing out, draining it and resuming—you know—everything is under vacuum. Nothing ever is open to air. It's a bit of a pain in the ass, but whatever. We can heat with hot water. We can boil with hot water. We don't need steam. And we had this big discussion, as [distillers] are going to find out, regarding fire.

Safety is always a major concern when designing a distillery. Regulators, now more conscious of the requirements and hazards of distilling, place more safety demands on new distilleries and are revisiting existing operations.

So the big worry is, let's say you have the still running. Pipes go, and you just dump all this ethanol vapor into the room. It could be scary. You dump it into the room, and you have a huge fire hazard—explosion hazard, really. With a vacuum you don't. And we do get leaks. It's very, very hard to get a perfect vacuum. So you're sucking in a little air. If you ever had a major problem, the still has to equalize first, and then it's not hot enough to boil. We're really going to stay on that because of the safety. It's just, you know, besides we'd have to have a steam boiler. Which we have one, but we've never hooked it up at the current building. And it's a major deal to hook up steam boilers. They're no joke. And that's the reality of getting into this business; there's a lot of equipment.

Distilling equipment requires a lot of space. Saxtons River recently acquired a thirteen-thousand-square-foot building, formerly a gymnastics gym, and transformed it into a new tasting room and production facility.

We're slowly accumulating new things. The idea with the move over here— everything is going to stay there [in the old distillery]. We're going to duplicate it. We're going to build a still—a slightly different design. How do we move over and shut everything down and rebuild it? We need to get everything here, and then we can shut things down and move it. We're busy enough that we need to get that running here before we can shut things down there. We have no time to shut everything down. The same, a new bottling line here and then we'll have two bottling lines.

We're also going to take on contract distilling. We have the space and then some. And I think there's going to be a value to it as people want to expand.

We talked, sitting on the floor, feet dangling off the edge of the former foam pit. Several feet below us, the floor resumed. The whole space was akin to an empty swimming pool, and it fit Christian's plan perfectly.

It's called secondary containment. I had a good discussion with Caledonia about their new expansion and build out. One of the things that's been a real headache for them is secondary containment. These tanks are getting big— one of our storage tanks is two thousand gallons. If that spills elsewhere, that's a problem. If that spills here, it's a swimming pool. I considered getting dock flotation and build[ing] a floor that essentially floated over this whole thing, and yet we'd have all this water for cooling, which is brilliant and would have been extremely difficult.

Ever the innovator, Christian chuckles as he unveils his latest idea: "One thing I want to try doing is videotaping [a distillation]. Because we distill at such a low temperature, we can put in a GoPro. Once. Those cases are acrylic. Alcohol would destroy it. Hopefully you could get the SD card out in time!

If anybody can do it, Saxtons River can.

SHELBURNE ORCHARDS DISTILLERY

Nick Cowles: *Owner/Distiller*

My grandfather died years ago, in 1986, in the old family house. After the service, there was a gathering at the house. I was standing in front of the hearth, and I noticed this knickknack of a bronzed dead bird. I was sitting there looking at it and thought, "What the hell?" And I felt a tap on my shoulder, and there was this old man. He goes, "I can tell you a story about that bird." Out of the blue this guy, he saw me staring at it. "That bird was found in the snow the morning after your grandfather's still caught fire during Prohibition." I didn't have much in common with my grandfather until that moment. I had been distilling since I was a teenager, and now my grandfather's dead. So I grabbed the guy by the elbow—"We need to sit down. I need to hear this story."[63]

Behind every great distillery is a great story. Nick Cowles is a practiced storyteller, a twinkle in his eye as he explains the origin of the name of his Dead Bird apple brandy.

It's the middle of the winter. It's below zero out. My grandfather's down in the cellar cooking up a batch of hooch—probably whiskey. It catches fire, and they have to call the fire department. The fire department shows up at the same time as the liquor control agent. The guys in the fire department were friends of my grandfather, so they knew about this stuff. The guy holding the hose goes "oops" and soaks the agent. It's so cold out the agent has to go home and change, and by the time he gets back, they've hidden all the evidence. Nobody gets caught that night. The next morning, there's a dead bird outside the cellar door that must have died from the smoke or whatever. My grandfather took it, had it bronzed, and he gave one to everyone in on it that night as a memento and a thank-you for keeping his ass out of jail.

Shelburne Orchards is a family operation that grows and sells a wide variety of apples and value-added apple products. The distillery exclusively produces aged apple brandy and pommeau, a delicious blend of apple brandy and fresh-pressed cider native to northwestern France.

I grew up here. It's my dad's orchard. I took over from him in the mid-'70s. I started planting some heirloom varieties in the mid-'80s, thinking—not thinking necessarily about brandy, but for hard cider and stuff. I've always been a little interested in hard cider. I love brandy and I love Calvados. And it was like, for years, thinking we'll never be able to make a good brandy with apples we're growing in Vermont. Or certainly, we'll never be able to make anything that tasted like French Calvados.

The Prohibition era did a number to the United States apple industry. Whereas many European growers still produce copious amounts and varieties of cider apples (apples with diverse levels of acid, sugar and tannin), the American apple industry remains largely dominated by dessert apples with high sugar levels and little structure.

I had a little hobby still since I was a teenager and was distilling apple cider, and at some point—well, we got our DSP in 2009. At some point prior to that, I started thinking, "Well, maybe we won't make necessarily anything that tasted like Calvados. Maybe we can find something." I had been planting different varieties. We had crab apples, all the heirloom varieties that were available…. "Maybe we can make something that's good, regardless if it's not like Calvados. But we can experiment with it."

Nick focuses on direct-to-consumer sales, with approximately 95 percent of sales happening right on the farm. As in-house sales increased, the utility of the packinghouse waned into obsolescence. It was the perfect opportunity to convert part of the farm into a distillery.

> *I was moving away from packing apples and selling all local. The packing line, I got rid of it. I dragged it out into the hedgerow, and this place opened up—this whole place opened up. And I said, "Whoa, this is the perfect situation." We've got the coolers, the forklift. All we've got to do is get a still and some fermentation tanks. There's floor drains. The cider press is right there. This is the perfect setup for a brandy operation.*

Nick pieced together the distillery from a variety of stills and tanks, an organic setup fitting for a farm-based facility.

> *I bought that [still] for $6,000 from Portugal. It showed up; I was so freaking pumped to see a copper still show up. I built the wood fire thing. It now runs on gas, but we started it on wood fire. We did it that way for the first three or four years until I got the other still. That I hooked up to gas and we realized how much easier it was to run on gas. It's a little more efficient to run it, keep it at just the right temperature. We can produce a barrel every two and a half days. We can fill a fifty-gallon barrel with 140-proof brandy. That's kind of my production. We have enough tanks. All my tanks are all different. All my tanks are these eclectic things; I found them all looking for deals and such. The orchard totally carried this since 2009. We started bottling last year.*

Nick begins fermenting during harvest, using apple seconds and multiple varieties to craft his blends.

> *I distill for December and half of January. That's my distilling season. I just run the stills for that time. We distill everything. We make it during the harvest. It takes approximately six weeks to ferment, less than that, but we let it go for six weeks....It's a great symbiosis, how it works with timing. We fill the tanks. Harvest is over. November I take off after harvest—well, not take it off but relax a little bit before distilling. I start the stills at four o'clock, 4:30. And we get done with the runs around 2:30 to 3:00 p.m. And we run them seven days a week for that six-week period of distilling time. Which is perfect. By the time we're done*

Nick carefully presses a
wax seal onto a bottle of
Dead Bird Apple Brandy.
*Courtesy of Shelburne
Orchards Distillery.*

*distilling this, I'm pretty sick of it and I don't want to get up at 4:30
anymore. It's a quality-of-life thing.*

Once it is distilled, Nick barrels the brandy and sets it aside for aging. It
will rest for a minimum of eight years.

*I filled ten sixty-gallon barrels this year. We started off the first year doing
four to six barrels, approximately. With the second still, we're now able to
do ten. And that fits my operation pretty well. The first barrel that I filled
in 2009, we filled it the day my grandson was born: December 6, 2009.
And that barrel we're not going to open until he turns twenty-one. He's just
turning ten this year.*

Secreted away in a dugout bunker, a carefully curated maturation program
guides the aging brandy from toasted oak to neutral oak, making sure the

spirit doesn't become too aggressive. The pommeau, a mix of two-year-old brandy and whatever fresh apples the orchard currently processes, is aged in oak for two to three years until mellow and clarified.

All the brandy goes into new Romanian oak, medium toast, for eighteen months. And then from there, after eighteen months, it is transferred into neutral barrels so it won't get over-oaked. Getting neutral barrels has been a challenge. I just bought twenty-four old French oak wine barrels that are considered neutral. I'm going to use those for pommeau first, and then the brandy will go in them. I'll do the new oak barrels three times—the first time eighteen months, and then twenty months, and then twenty-four months. And then they'll be considered neutral after three uses.

Apples are a notoriously expensive ingredient, a hurdle that makes brandy production cost-prohibitive for most distilleries. It is a costly endeavor, even for a vertically integrated distillery like Shelburne Orchards.

My costs are so much higher than people who are buying neutral grain spirits. They don't have to have the building, the distillery and all that stuff. Apple cider, if you think about it, is 6 percent alcohol. Cider is expensive!

Barrels of brandy and pommeau are meticulously labeled. *Courtesy of Shelburne Orchards Distillery.*

Corn is cheap sugar. It's a commodity. You can buy train car loads. It's harvested with huge equipment over acres with combines. Apples are picked by hand and are pressed in a cider press by hand. It's such a different deal. So my costs are way higher. I charge a hundred dollars per bottle. It's not too much. I'm not overcharging for what we make.

Visitors to Shelburne Orchards recognize the amount of work that goes into Dead Bird brandy and Nick's pommeau. Veteran and newfound patrons alike happily bring home a piece of Nick's story—a story of family, of farm and of a passion for distilled fruit.

People come in here. They're seeing the orchard. They know—a lot of my customers have been coming here for years. So they're buying a little bit of our heritage. They know me. They know the place. I hear, over and over again, this is the best Vermont gift to bring to someone. For Thanksgiving, they're taking it home to someplace. So there's that aspect. I think, for $100 a bottle, it's not going to be the drink that people drink every day. But if we're only going to bottle one thousand bottles, it's a little bit of an insurance program. It won't carry the whole business for a year, but one thousand bottles is a good shot in the arm.

SILO Distillery

Peter Jillson: *Co-Owner/CEO*
Erin Bell: *Head Distiller/Production Manager*

A farm-to-flask distillery located in Windsor, Vermont, SILO produces vodkas, gins, whiskeys and ciders from Vermont-grown ingredients. Built by Geobarns, a Vermont-based company, SILO's iconic red barn–distillery joins regional food and beverage favorites Harpoon Brewery, Vermont Farmstead Cheese Co., Artisan Eats Vermont and Blake Hill Preserves as part of Windsor's Artisans Park, an industrial park dedicated to craft production.

SILO Distillery was founded in 2013 by Peter Jillson, an eighth-generation Vermonter looking to return to his roots.

I wanted to get back to Vermont. I'm an eighth-generation Vermonter, and for a lot of people, they need to create their own destiny. When I was in the early stages, trying to figure out how that was going to happen for me versus being on a plane five days a week for thirty years, I was looking at the craft distilling industry, which was still in its infancy with a lot of great growth potential. We had a lot of the raw materials in our backyard. I was fortunate enough to go out and, through friends and family, was able to raise the initial monies to get us off the ground. It was daunting in the early days. The application process for federal licensing was a very uncomfortable piece of the puzzle, but we got through it and subsequently had to get another license for wine so we could do the hard cider. It's been an interesting ride.[64]

And so Peter made the jump. Having built a career out of developing marketing and sales teams for pharmaceutical, diagnostic and biotech companies—and spending countless hours traveling throughout the country—he returned home and began the transition into the wild world of craft distilling.

I was very lucky. Early on, I engaged in a friendship that is still ongoing—a guy named Monte Sachs. He owns Catskill Distilling over in Bethel, New York. Monte was very open to having me come over and spend as much time with him as I wanted. I went over there, took pictures. I took a couple courses in partnership with Cornell. And I stayed in touch with Monte. It would be six weeks into our distilling that I'd say, "Oh God, something's wrong." And he was there answering the questions I had. And I stayed in touch with him over time.[65]

Peter has a saying, one that his employees know well: "It's important to have everyone on the bus, on the right seats on the bus." Essentially, it's important that a business knows its employees and leverages their strengths and passions. Erin Bell, head distiller and production manager of SILO's all-female production team, never thought she'd find herself in the distilling industry but has proven herself a natural fit.

We've built the process from a lot of trial and error, and we have been fortunate that the right people have popped up at the right times. People ask me, "How'd you get into this?" I've no freaking clue. I got here by accident. I'm an accidental distiller. I was hired as a marketer who took over operations and firmly believes that you shouldn't have one person who knows how to do things. What happens if they get hit by a bus?[66]

SILO's iconic barn-distillery is a welcoming sight. *Courtesy of SILO Distillery.*

The process of creating a product from start to finish is different for every distillery, but it is nearly always a long, arduous task. SILO works with Jeff Grembowicz and Grembowicz Farm in North Clarendon, Vermont, from which SILO contracts non-GMO corn, rye and occasionally wheat. Jeff himself delivers grain to the distillery, where Erin's team moves each bag by hand to their hammer mill. They grind the grain, an augur carrying it up and into the mash tun. Direct-injected steam cooks the grain, and the mixture is transferred, solids and all, to fermentation tanks. After fermenting for a week, the fermented wash passes through the German-made Christian Carl still in a stripping run. Once low wines have been collected, the still is fired up again for a finish run. Vapor is directed through a tall column for vodka production or through a short column for whiskey, brandy and other more flavorful spirits.

> *We mostly work with Grembowicz Farm. I also just visited Andrew Peterson* [of Peterson Quality Malt], *who's great. He just has this really warm, welcoming presence. I saw his new malthouse, and wow! I'm going to get some malted wheat from him and more barley down the road. He's going to help me find some oats so we can play around with oats. Jeff's also working on finding oats. We work with Al Woods at Woods Syrup; that's where we source all our syrup from. He does barrel-aged syrups and also does syrup production. We work with Springmore Farm*

[in Baltimore, Vermont]. *They use our spent grain, and we usually try to get some cucumbers from them.*

We work with Curiosity Farm for cucumbers and maybe even a small batch of popcorn for a popcorn whiskey we're going to play around with. There's a lavender farm we've been talking to; we're not working with them yet. We just started working with Taza Chocolate and their winnowed cacao shells. We used to work with Lake Champlain Chocolates. And we work with Moore's Orchard in Pomfret for our cider.[67]

The relationships with Vermont producers are at the heart of Erin's production processes.

You can't work inside of a barn and not directly try to represent hardworking people. That's the nature of it. I've had a lot of people ask us recently, "There are a lot of craft distillers out there. What makes you unique?" It's a hard question to answer. I'm not going to turn around and tell you that we're doing something that hasn't been done before. People have been distilling for thousands of years. But I am going to tell you that the same values are intact across the board. The relationships are at the forefront. They come through in the products. The integrity is at the forefront. It comes through in the quality of the product. The few things that we do differently are really the longevity of those consistencies, those integrities and those relationships. And we've sustained them for six years now.[68]

SILO's diverse product line strongly represents its relationships with Vermont's agricultural economy. Vermont-grown corn provides the base for SILO Vodka, the flavored vodkas (SILO Cucumber, SILO Lavender and SILO Cacao) and SILO Gin, a refreshing sipping gin featuring juniper and Vermont-grown apples. Grembowicz Farm's rye joins the corn in SILO Bourbon, SILO Whiskey and SILO Maple, while Peterson Quality Malt's Vermont-grown, Vermont-malted barley stars in SILO Single Malt. Apples grown and pressed at Moore's Orchard in Pomfret, Vermont, are transformed into SILO's newest venture, hard cider.

Though its maturation program is small, SILO has experimented with a wide variety of barrels and woods. Early on, Peter used small ten-gallon and fifteen-gallon barrels from Black Swan Cooperage in Minnesota. The smaller barrels, their interiors honeycombed with grooves in order to accelerate aging chemistry, helped the distillery bring a quality aged product to market within a year of distillation. A limited run of SILO Aisling, a 100 percent wheat whiskey, utilized local charred ash wood staves in lieu of white oak. It drank similarly to a light Irish whiskey, slightly sweet with notes of almond and marshmallow. When the veteran-run Green Mountain Grain & Barrel launched in Richmond, Vermont, SILO was among its earliest supporters. Erin continues to work with Tony and Mac to restore old barrels and for new barrel inventory.

Peter affirms that the Vermont brand is an integral part of SILO's identity as a champion of local, field-to-flask production:

> *The Vermont cachet is massive. One of the great things about Vermont, and why the cachet is so strong, is that there's no corner-cutting. There are people out there who are cutting corners, but that will take care of itself. The consumer is becoming more and more educated. There are people in here every day who want to know where the grain comes from, what's the char in the barrel. It's a whole different level of conversation now, which is really cool. Everybody recognizes Vermont for food.*[69]

Much of SILO's production process is visible via a series of observation windows, and the staff readily answers questions about the ingredients and ongoing procedures. Communicating the story of the spirits, from grain to glass, is the core of SILO's philosophy.

Head distiller Erin Bell changes the still's vapor path. *Courtesy of SILO Distillery.*

Erin elaborates:

We're about consistency, integrity and relationships, from the farmer all the way to the bartender and customer, and the constant integration that happens there. That's the most important part. We do a lot of the things that we do because they're intentional. It's not because it's convenient. Sometimes it's not convenient at all. Sometimes it's more expensive. Sometimes we're just fortunate and people are really excited to work with us. Agriculture is extremely important, and it should be supported.[70]

Smugglers' Notch Distillery

Jeremy Elliott: *President/Co-Owner*

"I have this business because I wanted to live in this part of the country, in Vermont, and I wanted to raise my family here. I have a young boy and a beautiful wife. And that's how this started."[71]

Vermont has long been at the vanguard of the food and beverage industry, an active trailblazer of cottage production, craft brewing, artisan cheesemaking and, now, craft distilling. Today, in most cases, investors and legislators throughout the country recognize the burgeoning community of manufacturers, consumers and tradesmen that has arisen in support of craft spirits endeavors, and they welcome it. This wasn't the case in 2004, when Jeremy and his father, Ron, first started exploring the craft distilling industry. At that time, the industry was in its infancy, unknown and untested.

Back in 2002, I was working for a large pharmaceutical company. I was living in this town, Jeffersonville, and I was working for a company in New York. I was an R&D chemist. They announced they were shutting down the plant. Really, I wanted to still raise a family in Vermont. So, this is really young in the whole industry. I took a leave of absence from my job and called people out west. I said, "Hi, my name is Jeremy. Do you mind if I work with you for a month, month and a half, four- or six-week stints?" So I did a couple internships or apprenticeships. I did that for a year or two at a bunch of different places. Back then, the industry was so young. There were only a few small players. Now, flash forward to 2004 or 2006. I put everything together and said, "Do I want to open up a distillery or open up another company to synthesize APIs [active pharmaceutical ingredients]?" So I said, "Let's try distilling."

"Let's try distilling" is easier said than done, and Jeremy quickly found that investors were a bit skeptical of the fledgling industry. "I tried to raise money, raise capital. Nobody knew about this industry. So I tried to raise money. I was the keynote speaker at the Vermont Investors Forum. But everyone looked at me like I had three heads. Distilling?"

Jeremy had his father's support, however. Ron stood silently in the background of Jeremy's presentations, until one day...

Back in 2006, my dad came to me and said, "Man, Jeremy, you've been trying hard."

And I said, "Yeah Dad, I think this is a good path to go down, to follow."

I remember this conversation well. We were sitting on the patio outside at my place. It was dark. Bugs were coming out. And he said, "If you put in 50 percent, I'll put in 50 percent." And 50 percent was all I had. I was all in at that moment.

Smugglers' Notch Distillery was founded by father-and-son duo Ron (*right*) and Jeremy Elliott (*left*). *Courtesy of Smugglers' Notch Distillery.*

Jeremy and Ron started small, as many Vermont distillers do.

My father is my partner, my co-owner. He owns 50 percent of the business, and since that day, we've not had to raise any more capital. So our cap table is my father and myself. We started really small with a single still, two tanks, just a bulk tank and a blending tank. From 2008, we started making product, and I sold my first bottle of vodka in 2010. I still kept a full-time job up until 2016. That's another way we were able to grow. We didn't have any expenses; we were able to do almost everything ourselves. I was the graveyard shift, and my father was the day shift. And it was just the two of us for a long time.

Smugglers' Notch Distillery was not only one of the first distilled spirits plants (DSPs) in Vermont, but it was also among the first nationwide.

We were one of the very first people that came on board in the second wave. My DSP number is #2. Vermont Distillers [the original Vermont Distillers, makers of Tamarack Liqueur] *was probably before DSPs were a thing. I remember, when I got my DSP, I remember I was #171 in the whole U.S. And now, there's 2,500 to 2,600. It's crazy. We were one of the very first for the DSPs. We're at I think 23 or 24 here in the state. Not all are members of the DSCVT* [Distilled Spirits Council of Vermont].

Smugglers' Notch Distillery produces a wide variety of vodkas, gins, whiskeys and rums. "We make two gins. We make my original vodka and then an organic, gluten-free vodka. I have a bourbon and a maple bourbon that we were just working on this morning. Then a wheat whiskey and a rye."

Jeremy is upfront and transparent about his production processes, remarking on the necessities of contracting production and sourcing ingredients in order to maintain consistency and quality as Smugglers' Notch continues to grow.

All our grains come from Idaho. We've grown so big with our vodka production that I'm subcontracting my vodka production out so we can at least keep up until we can buy a larger still. I want to be fully transparent. I'd like to be all local. There's been a lot of feedback about what you do here, what you don't do here. I consider us to be a hybrid distillery. We're distilling and making stuff, and do I work with another company for the vodka? Yes, I do right now. It's the only way I can keep this place going, especially with the purchase of this new building. I always want to paint an accurate picture. My staff is trained to tell visitors the honest answer. That's how we live our lives and how we do our business. Would I like to be able to do it all in house? Absolutely. Would I like to use Vermont grains? I don't know. There are other regions of the country that grow a lot better grain. Everything we do use is sourced from a single farm in Idaho. We support American farmers, you know?

Jeremy uses a New England–made Trident still, an increasingly popular make among distillers in the Northeast. "We work with Trident Stills. Jesse's a great guy. I purchased one of the very first, first or second stills they made. We have an electric still. They got wired back up yesterday, after our move here [to this new building], but I have to get Jesse up here to help with things. He'll come down, have a beer with me and stay at my house."

Much of his other equipment and procedures are bespoke, largely inspired by Jeremy's past life in the pharmaceutical industry.

I think a lot of it is just using the right equipment and materials. A lot of that stuff is proprietary. For example, from as simple as fitting to the water we use. Everything has to be absolutely perfect. I learned a lot of that from the pharmaceutical industry. Tri-clamp fittings, whatever you have to do to ensure there's no contamination from any sort of plasticizers that will leach out. We only use stainless. Everything is food-grade, neat and clean. Everything has to be perfect. From the production side, I've learned a lot from my pharmaceutical experiences. I just absorbed everything. That makes us really unique—no plastics, nothing, perfect....I still to this day approve every single batch.

Properly educating staff and consumers alike is of the utmost importance to Jeremy's vision. In addition to the distillery tasting room in Jeffersonville, Smugglers' Notch also operates tasting rooms in Waterbury Center and Burlington.

We focus on education. We try to engage the consumers. We spend a lot of time with everyone who comes through our door, talking about spirits....I came up with three formulations for the first gin that we launched, and I crowdsourced it. We invited two hundred to three hundred people, and they chose the gin blend we currently make. So that was our first gin, our 802

*Gin. And I released the Hopped Gin two or three years later. The Hopped
Gin was actually the number-two winner for the same crowdsourcing.*

The educational initiative works well. Smugglers' Notch Distillery has
achieved significant growth in a relatively short amount of time.

"My whole goal is when someone goes into a store and they see a thousand
vodkas or bourbons, they know which one they want to pick up. Currently, as
of 2018, we've sold the largest amount of bottles in-state out of all Vermont
distillers. I'm proud of what we've accomplished over the last several years."

At the end of the day, however, it all comes back to family. As we say our
goodbyes and I move to leave, Jeremy stresses the importance of his father's
role in the company. Respect colors his voice:

*One more thing: I love working with my father. I never thought I'd be here.
One minute, we could be at each other's throats, screaming. Ten minutes
later, we've got to pick the phone back up and make a decision. It's great. It's
so cool. It's just—you've got to come right back and get it done. It's really,
really neat. I never thought we'd have a dynamic like this at this point in
our lives. Without him, I would have made so many mistakes along the way
and would have never gotten to where I am today.*

St. Johnsbury Distillery

Brendan Hughes: *Founder/President*
Dan Hughes: *Founder/Sales*
Duncan Holaday: *Founder, Duncan's Idea Mill, LLC*

St. Johnsbury Distillery, formerly known as Dunc's Mill, was purchased
in November 2017 from industry veteran Duncan Holaday by the St.
Johnsbury–based, father-son team of Dan and Brendan Hughes. Under
Holaday's mentorship, Brendan, Dan and the St. Johnsbury team continue
to produce the quality rums for which Dunc's Mill was known. Having
recently released their first of many original St. Johnsbury spirits, they are in
the process of moving distilling operations from Duncan's Barnet property
to a new facility on Eastern Avenue in St. Johnsbury.[72]

Brendan did not always want to be a distiller. In fact, for the longest time
he had his heart set on dentistry. "My whole way, from high school on, I

Featuring the ruby-throated hummingbird in its logo, St. Johnsbury Distillery specializes in producing quality New England rums. *Courtesy of St. Johnsbury Distillery.*

wanted to be a dentist. I went to school for biology in my undergrad, more in evolutionary biology—specifically in guppies, small fish in Trinidad and birds. You can see I'm using a lot of that now," he laughs. "That's actually why our logo has the hummingbird on it. The ruby-throated hummingbird is the only hummingbird native to this area of New England."

> *After graduation, I applied to a bunch of dental schools as well as this massive business program at the University of Notre Dame. Eventually, I realized that I was more interested in running my own practice, not really the dental work. So I chose the master's program and received a wealth of knowledge about start-ups. They tailored [the program] to coming up with your financials, finding funding, etc. Basically, they take the STEM students and if you come up with your own new technology, you'd be able to run with it as a business. It's really that fundamental start-up point they're teaching.*

Brendan spoke with his father, Dan, and the two decided to open a business together. Finding the brewing market too saturated, they looked to the Vermont Technical College distilling class, taught by none other than Duncan Holaday. Unfortunately, the class's dates coincided with Brendan's graduation. Undeterred, they gave Duncan a call.

So we reached out to Duncan and said, "Hey, we missed your class. We are very interested in this and were hoping to bounce ideas off of you." We had a meeting with him for two hours. He's an amazing guy. We really blended well with the whole relationship. Two weeks later, he contacted us and said, "Well, what do you think about buying us out?" That's the history of it.

While changes in ownership are typically a straightforward process, the name change from Dunc's Mill to St. Johnsbury Distillery brought with it some unforeseen consequences.

It would have been smooth sailing except that we changed the name. Even Duncan didn't really see it coming. Once you change the name, it's a new entity, so you can't assume all the permits that you had beforehand. That's one of the things we didn't realize going into it. We had a hiccup and received a cease-and-desist order in the beginning. We lost a lot of product.

Luckily, state legislators intervened on behalf of the distillery.

We had a lot of help from the legislators here. Senator Leahy jumped in and helped, too. That was more with the federal, the TTB, as well. They called down to Washington to get our permit all settled and happy again. There was a lot of help from Vermont, which was nice to see. Being able to start a business and help Vermont—you'll find that soft manufacturing is one of the faster growing sectors of Vermont commerce—it was nice to see the government stepping up to help us.

For Brendan, a St. Johnsbury native, maintaining a healthy relationship with local and state governments is of the utmost importance. "I was born and raised in St. Johnsbury. I wanted to move back to my hometown, so having an avenue like this to start with and run with, to really help the economy here by starting a business and creating jobs, is great. I was really excited to move back to my hometown and help it out."

"Naming our company St. Johnsbury Distillery is not by accident," Dan continues. "Across the country, the Vermont name has a very positive feel to it. Maybe people haven't even been to the state, but they like the concept.

You've got to have a good product, but we strongly believe that being in Vermont is an advantage."

A hometown operation—a tightknit group of family and friends producing high-quality goods—paints a perfect picture of the quintessential Vermont business.

Brendan says:

> *I'm more of the technical guy with the distilling, because of my background in biology and chemistry. Working in a laboratory setting, there's a lot of distilling that goes into chemistry. My dad is more the salesperson. He started a company here called Celtic Marketing, which is in the specialty food market. Companies like Cliff Bar hire my dad's company to sell their products on the East Coast. He's very much excited about that avenue. My brother-in-law—he also put money in—is the finance guy. He does a lot of the accounting and finance work. We're a really good three legs to the stool. We balance each other out well.*

Outside the family, Brendan teamed up with a couple of childhood pals.

> *Right now, we have two full-time employees. Part time we have about four. A lot of them are college students who come in the summer. When we're doing farmers' markets and everything like that, we've got a lot of part-time employees. Otherwise, we have Mark, who's the distilling and manufacturing manager, more that technical side. His background is in engineering. It's nice to have a guy who can work on the still. We also have Greg, who is taking on the role of sales and marketing manager. We're all high school buddies, and it's nice to work on something together. Greg does help with the distilling as well, and I do too, but the majority of his time is spent going to bars, keeping his feet on the ground, going to Massachusetts for tastings, you know.*

Together with the help of Duncan Holaday, the team at St. Johnsbury Distillery continues the Dunc's Mill legacy of producing spirits from start to finish. Currently operating out of the original Dunc's Mill distillery, a largely vertical production space located adjacent to Holaday's home in Barnet, Vermont, they look forward to the new production facility and the small luxuries it will bring—access to a forklift, for example.

> *The initial mash is put into our fermenters up here. Hammering out the sugar cane down there, mixing it with water, making sure it's a good*

combination of the two. Feeding it up—in the new facility, it will be better because we can gravity feed it, but for now we're pumping it up. We inherited two fermenters, and we brought in the other two to help out with our manufacturing time. From here, we can gravity feed into the still right here. There are a lot of avenues for taking cuts, feeding it down there to our 250-gallon tank. This is doing our first and second cut. We're able to do that because of the different cutoff points we're putting into the still.

The still, custom designed by Duncan, is a complex, brilliant work of art. Brendan explains:

It's designed for product that we have now. That's why the rum we produce is of a higher quality, because of the process he went into in designing the still we're using. We just purchased another still that we'll be using in our new facility that we're building on Eastern Avenue. The new still will be mostly used for the first cut. We do double-distill our rum, which is peculiar for a rum, but we find it really isolates the high-quality alcohol that we want.

Joining us at the distillery, Duncan adds:

It has two heads. That one comes off. That one swings down. That's one of my inventions—it's the water flow condenser. You use the cold plate and create sort of waterfalls. The vapor tries to go through the waterfalls. And it works. The vertical system makes sense. You never want to have to pump ethanol or carry it around. That's why it should be vertical, coming down, down, down to the bottle. We're working on that model.[73]

Brendan continues:

Because of the water control that Duncan incorporated into [the still], you're able to really cut off the points more precisely between the heads, the mids and the tails. It's an integrated system of a lot of valves to control the water. It's got a mad scientist/genius aspect to it, and it's really cool. He also designed the one at Vermont Spirits. He was one of the founders of that company as well. You'll see similarities between the two stills; they're basically sisters.

In the beginning, Duncan experimented with several products whose foundations were rooted firmly in Vermont agriculture.

I had used just about every substrate, and I've helped people do other things—beets, whatever. I'd worked with maple first, pure maple, and that's a ridiculous model. The guy who started WhistlePig was also involved with us for a little while. He said, "These should be $125 a bottle," and he was absolutely right....I didn't want to do that again. But I love sugaring. These guys enjoy it too. And I had worked with milk, making milk vodka. You never want to try to make alcohol out of milk. Milk wants to be cheese. It wants to be yogurt. But it doesn't want to be alcohol. So I wrestled with that and started doing it. It was just too difficult, although I was getting free whey from Cabot cheese.[74]

Finally, he settled on sugar cane and rum production.

I loved working with cane. It wants to be alcohol. You throw it on the floor and it becomes alcohol. So I said, "That's what I want to do." And I'm sugaring and I love maple. So I just automatically came up with the idea of maple rum. It's a natural marriage, and I did it well. I didn't fuss around with it. I just used the basic ingredients, and it came out well.[75]

St. Johnsbury Distillery continues to make Dunc's Maple Rum, Dunc's Elderflower Rum and Backwoods Reserve Rum, and it has recently released its own product, Brendan's Spiced Rum. Brendan describes their newest addition:

We just launched the first new [rum] under our name, which is the Brendan's Spiced Rum, named after Saint Brendan the Navigator, who allegedly discovered America before Christopher Columbus. So that's kind of the tagline story on the bottle. It's a good twist on a traditional spiced rum. A lot of times they have that vanilla-flavored background, but ours has more citrus. You'll taste the Jamaican-infused spices to begin with, and it will finish like you've just eaten an orange. It's really refreshing, really cool. Going through the whole R&D process was an amazing experience, especially with Duncan. We came up with a really great product and are really proud of it.

New England has a beautiful, storied history with rum, and it's refreshing to witness St. Johnsbury Distillery as it continues its deep dive into all it has to offer. Brendan concludes, "We're exclusively rum for right now. We're probably going to stay that way, stick to what we know. In the future, we may branch out, but for now, we're solely rum."

STONECUTTER SPIRITS

Sivan Cotel: *Co-Founder/Director of Operations*

Distillery co-founder Sivan Cotel dives into the Stonecutter Spirits story:

We are a woman-led craft distillery, and we are very proud of that. That's a unique thing in an industry that has been very heavily male-dominated. I'll say personally as the male half of our duo, that I love that. It's amazing the way that Sas [Stewart] excels in the parts of our business that I don't [excel at]. That's why we're a team. I'm the logistical side of things. I am business planning, operations and financial management. She is the vision side of things. She is vision and strategy and branding and where-do-we-take-this-thing? It's because of Sas that we are actually thinking of what we are going to do next.[76]

Social innovation and the avant-garde are notions that have become synonymous with Stonecutter Spirits, the Middlebury-based distillery known for its impressive maturation program and inspired consumer engagements.

We are five years in now. And when we started the vision was really to use custom, different or unique aging techniques to make spirits that are truly special. And we didn't want to do every spirit under the sun. There's nothing wrong with folks that choose that model, but that's not the model for us. We were interested in doing the things that (a) we could make a difference and do something that wasn't already being served, whether we felt it was a specific opportunity or a niche that could be explored, and (b) things that we, ourselves, are very interested in.

Before the advent of Stonecutter Spirits, Sivan was the COO and CFO of WhistlePig Whiskey. After two years with the well-known, Vermont-based whiskey company, he began consulting for other distillery startups.

I helped clients plan out their aging models, which is one of my specialties. People might have business sense or have taken a distilling class. But how do you balance it? If you don't lay enough down, you've capped your growth. If you lay too much down, you're wasting your capital, burning your balance sheet. That's one of the biggest things I was brought to WhistlePig to do. I was planning out a fifteen- to twenty-year aging ladder. What do you have in barrels now? What is it allocated towards? How do you put more down?

With a graduate degree in urban environmental systems and a decade in fine dining under her belt, Sas consulted for small food and beverage businesses and hoped to start a co-working space in Middlebury.

> We started thinking about what could we do together, and this idea took off pretty quickly. We started working on the business on paper, speccing it out, before we moved on it. Then we started looking for space. And I think early on if X, Y and Z hadn't have happened, we would have pulled the plug. And one of the big ones was finding this space we're in right now. Sas was working on a separate project at the time, trying to start a co-working space in Middlebury. She came back one night and said, "I found a space that is super wrong for co-working, but it's so right for what we're talking about. You're going to love it." It was a twelve-thousand-square-foot space with no internal walls. We got to cut it up how we wanted it. It already had local and state permitting. It already had good water and a loading dock. It was the blankest of canvases you could want, and the landlord is lovely.

Building secured, the duo started the product development process, working first on a gin and then finding a supply of whiskey.

Sivan Cotel (*left*) and Sas Stewart (*right*), co-founders of Stonecutter Spirits, showcase their Single Barrel Gin and Heritage Cask Whiskey. *Courtesy of Stonecutter Spirits.*

We immediately started working on gin recipe development. Half a year later, we started on whiskey recipe development, but we also started looking at sourcing aged whiskey to build out our pipeline. We do believe it's okay to source whiskey as long as you're transparent about it. And that's an important qualifier for us. I think a lot of folks do believe that now as well, whether they believe that because they have to, because customers demand it or because they want to. In the end, much of the industry has moved towards transparency in sourcing, for whatever the motivation.

A Good Food Awards recipient and winner of a Double Gold medal at the San Francisco International Spirit Awards, Stonecutter's carefully crafted Single Barrel Gin was the first product released by the distillery.

The whole goal for us was to create a gin that was lightly aged. For us, aging is not a different category. A lot of folks talk about aged gin versus gin as different categories. We view aging as a technique to make the gin more special. We don't view it as an aged gin. And for us, that freed us up to think about it a little differently rather than making it just "whiskey-like." A lot of aged gins are, probably by accident or maybe on purpose, are more like whiskey than might be properly balanced. I think we were really fortunate to hit it on the nose.

Sivan continues:

Our gin is lightly golden, not dark brown. And I don't mean that for the aesthetic point. I mean that for what it implies about the aging and the nuance that we are able to get from that. It's about nuance; it's not about being oaky. For us, that's been a wonderful chance to make something different. It gave us a chance to explore botanicals in a certain way. We are able to think about the barrel and aging as part of our recipe even though it comes later in the process.

Stonecutter's Single Barrel Gin is a great example of the intricacies of maturation. Rather than a blunt instrument with which to add color and flavor, Sivan speaks of the more delicate and intentional interactions that take place within the barrels.

It was about leaving room for the elements you get from the barrel. Leaving room for the vanillas and caramels you get naturally from that bourbon barrel. The other aspect that has been very lovely to see as it's developed, just knowing our recipe very well, is to see how some of the botanicals—and I don't know how to describe this from a scientific perspective—recombine during the aging process in ways that are really lovely. For example, one of our major botanicals is cardamom. One of our minor botanicals is green tea. The way those two are married in the barrel is very cool. It is noticeable how they are each a little more subtle and influenced by each other during the aging process.

At Stonecutter Spirits, aging is more than just a number. Sas and Sivan push the boundaries of maturation, exploring the nuances of finishing barrels and striving to redefine notions of what whiskey is, was and can be. The Heritage Cask Whiskey, Stonecutter's second product, was born in this light.

The same idea carried through when we look at whiskey. What other opportunities can be explored? With whiskey, it was again about using barrels differently. To have a bourbon-style recipe but to intentionally say, "We're not using new barrels; therefore, we're not going to be able to call it bourbon." And we're not making the decision from a marketing and branding perspective that we want to make it bourbon because that's a more easily understandable category. We're making the decision based on what we think is a niche that can be filled of something that is an opportunity in booze, and we'll figure out how to convey to folks what it is, even though that's the challenge. And so we do a whiskey that is aged in three barrels— two former bourbon barrels in succession and then former cabernet barrels.

The use of wine barrels has always interested Sivan, who sees their use as an opportunity to bridge gaps between consumers.

I've always been interested in wine barrels and the cousins of wine— the fortified wines, Marsala, port, sherry. We really felt there was an opportunity with something like that. We're not the first to ever use different barrels, but certainly I feel that what we're doing is a little different. It is amazing how when you're talking to a customer while they taste it, someone whose palate is mostly refined by their experiences with bourbon experiences it as a cousin of bourbon. Someone whose palate is refined by Scotch experiences it as a cousin of Scotch. And those who drink Irish see it as Irish. And it has something in common with all of those, right?

It's a bourbon-style recipe, aged like an Irish whiskey and finished like a Scotch....It's cool to see how people connect with it, because then they will connect it back to their basic traditions.

Rather than aging every barrel separately and blending them together at the end—a common practice—every drop of Stonecutter's whiskey experiences time in each barrel type.

Stonecutter Spirits is known for the innovative ways in which it engages consumers, such as its Adventure Dinner series. These pop-up, speakeasy-style cocktail dinners are designed and hosted by Stonecutter. Featuring a diverse cast of Vermont producers, they're frequently held in remote locations or are secreted away in seemingly vacant urban hideaways. Invitations are sent out when new dinners are planned, and seats are limited. Once reserved, patrons are cryptically reminded to remain vigilant. "Be prepared to be on your toes," warns Stonecutter's website. "RSVP to a dinner and you'll get the exact starting location texted 24 hours before the event."

In addition to the Adventure Dinners, Stonecutter has also opened up Highball Social, a satellite bar and tasting room located in Burlington.

It [Highball Social] *is meant to be a really immersive experience where someone can connect with what makes Stonecutter really cool without being an in-your-face branding experience. It is our space. And it is cocktails with us. We just want to share with people all the cool things we do. We built the bar and restaurant we want to hang out in. And we built a custom hi-ball machine that is styled off the Japanese whiskey hi-ball machine. It hyper-chills the spirit, whiskey on one side, gin on the other, and then carbonates that spirit while chilled. That comes through the tap lines either with soda water for the whiskey hi-ball, or the gin one is with a custom soda that savouré soda in Bristol made for us which has cardamom, lovage and celery. So we have these delightful whiskey hi-balls or gin hi-balls which have these delightful tiny champagne-style bubbles.*

Stonecutter's creativity doesn't end with its customer interface. Its aging warehouse has also been carefully designed. Light tubes provide the majority of ambient light, supplemented with highly efficient LED panels. The floors and walls are treated with an industrial zero-VOC (volatile organic compounds) coating. Both the whiskey and gin are kosher certified, a process that speaks to intentionality and precision, and the warehouse's temperature and humidity are uniquely monitored.

In the warehouse, we are intentionally pulling air flow in every day—little bits or more on timers every day. We have two inputs up high up there, and then we have two out on fans on explosion proof dampers, and they are on timers. They can run fifteen minutes a day or a couple hours, depending on what we need. We pull in fresh air every day. We pull the same temperature and pressure variations you get naturally outside, in here. So you get both generally, seasonally variation of temperature and pressure, but also throughout the day variations on temperature and pressure. And with that we are getting our barrels to expand and contract every day and a little bit over the season. We are getting more robust interactions between the spirit and the wood of the barrel. We think of that as our Vermont terroir.

Terroir. It's a term most frequently associated with wine and cheese, products more commonly and directly associated with regional agricultural processes. In particular, the term *terroir* refers to the characteristic flavors imparted to a product by the environment in which it is grown. "The taste of place" is a central theme of Stonecutter Spirits, from the careful curation of its warehouse climate and the social climates of its events and tasting rooms to the very name of "Stonecutter," a representation of Middlebury, Vermont's history.

Middlebury, Vermont, historically was a marble quarry. That was the main economy of the town. So Sas and I were trying to hit on something that would be tied to the history here without being in your face about it. We wanted something that someone could connect with, that was still tied to here, but could also be as meaningful to someone in California as here in Vermont. So we were really happy when we found the idea of Stonecutter, because it ties to the history here and in a much broader way if you think about it—well, the original economy of this town disappeared. This town endured. Different economies came up and became a part of it. Stone masonry and stonecutting were part of the original artistic economy. There's a lot of creativity in those skill-based economies. You look at something like distillation or the alcohol movement in general—beer, wine—those are very artistic, creative, technical industries. So it felt very thematically appropriate to us.

Vermont Distillers

Ed Metcalfe: *Founder/President*

Located in Marlboro, Vermont, Vermont Distillers' distillery and tasting room sports an incredible view of the historic Hogback Mountain Ski Area. The slopes, now largely reclaimed by nature, are a perfect symbol of Vermont's celebrated narrative as a paragon of natural history and outdoor recreation.[77]

Run by Ed Metcalfe and his two sons, Gus and Dominic, Vermont Distillers is best known for its family of liqueurs, sweet and sippable portrayals of maple syrup, raspberries, blueberries and peaches. In addition to these fruit-laden cordials, Ed, Gus and Dom also produce a seasonal limoncello and the 100 percent corn-based Catamount Vodka.

For Ed, working with fruit-forward alcoholic beverages was nothing new.

It was 1981. I was making a little over $8,000 a year as a teacher. A friend offered me a job making $15,000 a year managing a liquor store that he bought. So I moved down to Rhode Island and managed a store down there for a couple years. Eventually, I worked as a salesman for Sakonnet Vineyards—kind of their sole sales force going around the state. It's a small state, so it was easy to do. So I got this idea that I wanted to start a winery, and Vermont was the only state at the time that didn't have a winery. I moved back north and started making plans. I did that in 1985; North River Winery we called it. It was the only winery in the state. It was in the village of Jacksonville down in Winingham. We made fruit wines. We started doing some grape stuff, but the fruit wines took off.

North River Winery was successful, reaching a production of approximately 4,500 cases per year. Ed sold the business in 1997 and took a short break from the alcohol industry.

I sold the winery in 1997. I always had in the back of my mind that I wanted to do something different. In 2007, I wrote a business plan for a distillery. I entered it in a business plan competition in Brattleboro and won 1,000 bucks. Another year went by, and I entered it again in 2008 and won first prize—ten grand. At that time, 2008, North River Winery was folding. The guy who bought it from me was going out of business. So I bought tanks and stuff—you know, like a dollar and a quarter per gallon of stainless....It was all based on the idea of doing a maple cream liqueur and a maple liqueur. In 2012, I really got started making the maple cream liqueur and the raspberry liqueur. [Until recently] *we always purchased ethanol and blended; we weren't doing any distilling.*

The flagship Metcalfe's Maple Cream Liqueur is 17 percent alcohol-by-volume and is a comforting blend of cream and maple syrup, similar to an Irish cream liqueur. The Maple Liqueur, at 30 percent ABV, is a more spirit-forward blend of corn-based distillate and maple syrup.

Rectifying and blending is a cost-effective way for young distilleries to produce and bottle product without the costly capital and labor investment inherent in running a still. Several Vermont distilleries, including Vermont Distillers, began as rectifiers and processors and moved to (or intend to move to) in-house distillation once the numbers worked.

We bought a still a year and a half, two years ago. We had all kinds of problems with the still—some were basic problems with the still. But the state electrical inspector I got really knew his stuff, to a point where all the electronics—it is an electric still—he didn't like any of it. And an

Ed Metcalfe (*center*) and sons Gus (*left*) and Dominic (*right*) of Vermont Distillers. *Courtesy of Vermont Distillers.*

electrician friend of mine said, "You know, he's got a good point. This and this and this and this…" So it took us the better part of a year to get our still straightened out. We had a small electric panel. Now we have one two or three times bigger.

With the still in operating order, Ed stayed true to his roots and brought in 4,800 gallons of sweet apple cider. Fermented and distilled on site at Vermont Distillers, Ed will experiment with the results until he finds a product that works within their current portfolio. Some may be barreled, and some may be blended.

"The thing that I learned at the winery—everyone says they love dry wines because that's what they're taught to say, but in reality everyone buys sweet wines. Our best-selling wine at the winery was a raspberry-apple wine. So that's where I went with this [Vermont Distillers]. And it works really well in the tasting room."

In addition to the tasting room located at the distillery, Vermont Distillers also operates a tasting room on Church Street in Burlington. Shared with Smugglers' Notch Distillery, the distilleries benefit greatly from the foot traffic of Burlington's pedestrian shopping district.

Other future Vermont Distillers endeavors include experiments with bourbon and seasonal, limited-release products such as Ciriaco's Limoncello (named after Gus and Dom's grandfather Ciriaco Cardone). A cult-favorite garlic vodka makes an exclusive appearance at the annual Southern Vermont Garlic and Herb Festival.

We sold over $8,000 of booze at the garlic festival. [People] two or three deep the whole time we were there. We made a garlic vodka for that, which is kind of interesting. We made it for the festival two years ago and sold a little bit of it but had a bunch left over. We didn't sell a lot of it at the festival—mostly our other stuff. We brought it back—the stuff had changed significantly over a year, and it was so much smoother!

"Vermont Distillers" is a valuable brand name, one that existed long before Ed started his distillery. It was the name of Vermont's "first" modern craft distilling operation, launched in 1989 just outside Waterbury, Vermont. While still running his winery, Ed collaborated with Vermont Distillers to distill an off-batch of pear wine. He acquired the name after the original Vermont Distillers closed.[78]

> *There was one* [distillery] *called Vermont Distillers which was back when I had my winery. They were in Waterbury. A guy named Steve Israel was one of the principals. I had a pear wine that went bad on me. It went bad in such a way that I thought it could be distilled. I had it trucked up there—we had 2,500 gallons of it—it had undergone a bacterial infection that gave it a lot of…strong acetic acid but no ethyl acetate. It didn't smell like vinegar. It smelled beautiful, but it tasted awful. So we brought it up there, and they distilled it. They had all these barrels of beautiful pear-smelling distillate. They then went out of business. I was under the impression then that I couldn't even have it at my winery. And the stuff ended up a state warehouse, and I don't know what happened to over two hundred gallons of a really great pear distillate.*

Who knows? Now that Vermont Distillers has its still up and running, maybe Ed, Gus and Dom will re-create that beautiful pear-smelling distillate, bringing it all full circle.

Vermont Spirits

Steve Johnson: *President/CEO*

Hailed as Vermont's oldest distillery, Vermont Spirits celebrated its twentieth anniversary in May 2019. Founded by Vermont distilling veteran Duncan Holaday in 1999 at his home in Barnet, Vermont, the company moved its entire operation—equipment, building and all—to Quechee, Vermont, in 2011. Now located in the Quechee Gorge Village alongside the tasting rooms of Putney Mountain Winery and the highly esteemed Cabot Creamery, Vermont Spirits continues its production of innovative, agriculturally inspired spirits.[79]

Steve Johnson, president and CEO of Vermont Spirits, joined the team in 2006 as the distillery sought to broaden distribution.

> *I came into the business in the middle of 2006. I was introduced to the company through a friend who knew one of Duncan's friends. Immediately, he put me to work in negotiating a distribution deal with Anheuser-Busch when they were getting into spirits back in 2006–7. I think they ended up doing half a dozen deals with small distilleries. So I started that, and*

in 2007, I came on full time as head of marketing. I had no distilling experience before that. I had spent ten years in journalism, worked in banking and owned a few small businesses prior to that—a slate company up here, a mix of stuff. With the Anheuser-Busch transaction, I came on board working with Duncan and his staff, just beginning distribution. The company hadn't done much with distribution other than in Vermont and New Hampshire until that time.

While new to the spirits industry at the time, Steve was not a total stranger to the distilling process. "My dad's side, my family in Hungary, did distilling as a kind of hobby. My grandfather grew tobacco, and his sons made some local booze for home use."

The centerpiece of Vermont Spirits' operation is a gorgeous twenty-four-foot-tall glass column still designed by Duncan Holaday. It is supported by two additional 150-gallon stills. Steve explains, "We make everything. We find parts and use local fabricators for the work. The bigger still was never used in the old place, but the smaller one was. With the dairy business in the state, [fabricators] can work with stainless really well. At some point we should probably upgrade, but to this point it has worked really well for us."

The trio of stills produces a wide variety of spirits using botanicals and fermentable ingredients sourced, when feasible, from Vermont.

We try our best to use local ingredients when possible. We handpick the juniper in Vermont in the fall and try and source everything from the state if we can, as much as possible. Maple we get from one co-op. We used to tap our own trees, but now we buy it by the tote. For our VS Limited Release Vodka, we partner with a different maple producer each year. This year it's Amber Ridge Maple way up north. We got a really nice batch of early sap from them. The berries we get from some local farms here. For apples, we work with Eden Cider a fair bit. We sell stuff for Eleanor and use their aperitif cider in our 1791 Barrel-Aged Cocktail. Obviously not everything grows here, but we try to get everything we can here in Vermont.

Vermont Spirits began production with a suite of three unique vodkas that continues to receive attention for its distinct ingredients and noteworthy flavors. "We have Vermont Gold, which is made from maple. Then we have Vermont White, which is made from lactose and milk sugars. And then VS Limited Release, which is distilled from early run sap—we had a really good batch this year."

Known as a pioneer of maple-inspired spirits—in addition to its Vermont Gold and VS Limited Release vodkas, Vermont Spirits also utilizes maple in its No. 14 line of bourbon, apple brandy and aged maple spirit—the distillery also receives considerable attention for its whey-based Vermont White Vodka. Reminiscent of historical clarified milk punch, a velvety cocktail of sorts common to colonial England and its American colonies, the successes of Vermont White came not without its fair share of challenges.

The whey vodka is a tough one to sell. It's interesting. People are curious when they taste it. If you don't tell them what it is, they think it's great. It's always a hard one to make a connection between milk and getting to vodka. Then what do you mix it with? We once won an award for having the best vodka for a Bloody Mary. But you can't really taste it. If people thought about milk, tomato juice and lemon, it's kind of like curdling in your stomach and not the best image. But it's a great, classic, versatile vodka for a martini or vodka tonic. It works beautifully. There are a few other distilleries making it in the U.S. now. There are one or two gins I've seen, so people are trying it.

From vodka, Vermont Spirits diversified into gins, whiskeys and beyond.

Gin is a fairly easy step to start making from vodka. Harry [Gorman, distiller of Vermont Spirits] *really wanted to try making it. We had some fits and starts. Our first gin was released, and it did okay. I pulled it off the shelf in the state because I wasn't happy with it. We jiggered the formula a bit and rereleased it, and now it does really well. We've received a lot of awards for* [Coppers Gin]. *We have a barrel-aged gin and one called Sugarwood, where we add a little maple syrup to it. With bourbon taking off, it was easy for us to add that and put our Vermont twist on it by finishing it off, again, with maple syrup.*

Many of Vermont Spirits' products are seasonally produced or seasonally inspired.

It's pretty easy to make a liqueur. Every spring we have a batch release. We also have an apple brandy which we make periodically. Brandy is a lot of work. And then we have our Maple Spirit. It's kind of like a brandy, but the TTB doesn't allow us to call it that because brandy is not a commodity type. We start it the way we make our vodka then take it off the still at a higher proof and barrel-age it for a couple years. It's quite nice.

Finally, Vermont Spirits bottles a barrel-aged cocktail. Named 1791 after the year Vermont joined the United States, it's an easy-drinking marriage of rye, cranberry and honey. "Normally the entire cocktail is aged a month to three months in oak. I figured it would be something for the fall, but it has turned out to be popular in the spring and summer. We work with Eden Iced Cider. They provide the apple aperitif for [1791]. It's taken off and become one of the biggest sellers here at the store."

As the oldest distillery in the state, Vermont Spirits stands as a testament to the innovation and persistence of Vermont's distilling industry.

> *Everybody is making great stuff, being creative and trying to push the industry along from its dated roots. I think we're known for being the first to produce distilled spirits using maple syrup. I give Duncan credit for that idea way back then, and I have continued that trend since I took over ten years ago. It hasn't been without challenges, ups and downs, but we've been here for twenty years.*

Steve laughs. "We have to be doing something right."

WHISTLEPIG WHISKEY

Peter Lynch: *Master Blender*
Emily Harrison: *Distillery Manager*

There are distilleries, there are farm distilleries and then there are estate distilleries. The WhistlePig Whiskey farm complex rushes to meet you as you emerge, rumbling down a dirt road, from the wooded hills that surround the property. Greeted on one side by a rustic sugar shack and on the other by a well-kept farmhouse, it is hard to ignore the splendor of the barn-red buildings before you. Each has a distinct purpose, an individual cog in the great, whiskey-producing apparatus that is WhistlePig.[80]

Master blender Peter Lynch sets the scene further, framing the context of WhistlePig's origin story:

> *The distillery proper is a renovated 150-year-old dairy barn. This property was purchased in 2007 with really no vision whatsoever. Eventually, we realized our dream in 2009–10. We started sourcing whiskey from Canada*

in order to release our first product, a 10-year [whiskey]. The goal with this barn itself and with the property was to create a farm-to-glass distillery here in Vermont: growing our own grain on these fields around us, using water from our well, distilling on site, using Vermont oak in production as well. It took us a bit longer than expected because of legislation, in a sense. All kinds of environmental studies had to be done. A lot of money had to be spent. A lot of time had to be taken. Eventually, we finally got all our permits in and whatnot. The still arrived in 2015. We've been distilling since 2015. We've been producing whiskey since about 2009–10, and we have grown explosively since then.

Peter continues:

The ten-year [whiskey] is our flagship. This is what we rest our hat on. It's ten years old, 100 proof, straight rye, with a very high rye content. It's blended from a couple different distilleries in Canada, finding all the best qualities of different rye whiskeys. It's big. It's bold. It stands up to cocktails. We like to think of ourselves as innovators, too. We push the fold, whether by age statement or by cask finishes and experimentation, which you can see in our twelve-year product.

A stroll through the old dairy barn reveals a series of product displays. Reminiscent of a county fair exhibition, they outline the progression of WhistlePig's distilling history. Peter describes each whiskey with pride:

Our twelve-year was the result of barrel finishing experimentation. We took the whiskey out of its original barrel and put it into various ex-wine, ex-spirit casks. This whiskey was the result of one of those experiments where we settled on Madeira, Sauterne and port casks being the perfect three for marriage. We finished this twelve-year-old rye whiskey from Indiana in these three casks and marry them in these set percentages to get a nice blend going.

As Peter spotlights whiskey after whiskey, the story behind each spirit becomes more elaborate, one step closer to realizing WhistlePig's vision of an estate-made spirit.

The next logical step in our aging and terroir evolution was our fifteen-year [whiskey], which was the next product we released. Fifteen-year is fifteen

Master blender Pete Lynch tackles maturation at WhistlePig Whiskey. *Courtesy of WhistlePig Whiskey.*

years old and 100 percent rye, coming out of one distillery in Canada. Huge classic, bold rye flavors, 92 proof—it carries that weight with it as well. What's unique about it is that it is the first employment of Vermont estate oak. We've been harvesting oak from the area around the farm—we only have so many trees around here—and from throughout Vermont. We send those trees down to the Independent Stave Company, who makes pretty much all the barrels for the whiskey makers in the U.S. Vermont oak, having a much different growing season than the Ozark Mountain range (which is typically where the wood for our whiskey barrels come from), has a much tighter grain. It gives a lot of flavor a lot more quickly. It's like a French oak barrel. So we're basically able to enhance this whiskey, infuse the flavor of Vermont oak into it and give it this extra layer of a bold, oaky backbone.

The next iteration of WhistlePig Whiskey was Farmstock, a whiskey crafted to feature WhistlePig's estate-distilled spirit. An answer to the ever-growing demand for a house-distilled product, Farmstock evolves year to year. Each new "crop" released by the distillery is slightly different, slightly older and features an increased amount of estate-distilled whiskey. Peter concludes with Boss Hog, a special release product:

Last but not least is Boss Hog. This is one of our favorite products. It's our once-per-year limited release. This is our biggest, boldest, not necessarily oldest, but best whiskey at cask strength with a unique finish on it. Something that makes you say, "Oh, yeah." We've had various versions of it throughout the years. This is where we push the line with innovation. We started releasing these in 2013. First we just released these big, bold, delicious cask-strength whiskeys with a lot of flavor. We then worked with finishing. Boss Hog Three had a very interesting barrel finish. It was a de-charred, re-charred Islay barrel. It had an interesting smoky Scotch finish. Boss Hog Four, which won best in show whiskey at a San Francisco World Spirits competition, was finished in Armagnac casks. Boss Hog, the fifth edition, was finished in Calvados barrels, which gives it a nice apple-y sort of flavor. This is one of the pride and joys of WhistlePig, especially among the production team.

WhistlePig also recently released Piggyback, a younger rye whiskey at a lower price point, designed to withstand the rigors of cocktail construction. At six years old and 100 percent rye, it's dedicated to Dave Pickerell, WhistlePig's late master distiller.[81] Peter adds:

This is in a way Dave Pickerell's last hoorah and a shout-out to him, in a sense. Dave always loved the bartending community—for what they've done for him, not just for WhistlePig but for the industry in general. He loved traveling around and making friends. Before Dave passed, we had Piggyback in production and were working on it. We decided to dedicate it to him. The pig, our logo, has his Stetson hat on instead of the bowler. The proof is 95.56; his birth year is 1956.

WhistlePig Farm has five hundred acres of tillable land and grinds its estate-grown grain in the Church Mill, an appropriately named millhouse in the form of an old country chapel. It bottles product in its centrally located production area, a largely manual process involving several individuals and a manually fed conveyer system.

Peter smiles as he recalls the trials and tribulations of starting out small:

The Church Mill used to be this crappy, rusted-over iron hut semicircle-type thing. It was not fun to mill grain here over the summertime. As we had success out in the market and world, we looked back on ourselves at the farm and said, "We can build silos, get a better milling system and proper bottling equipment." One of the things we pride ourselves on is that we're totally hand bottled. But even small things like a conveyor system have been useful. To put it in perspective: the first rounds of WhistlePig, the first several rounds, were hand-bottled by Middlebury College interns using graduated cylinders and coffee filters. On picnic tables. They'd spill it everywhere.

In the distillery portion of the old dairy barn, two large copper stills take center stage. Emily Harrison, WhistlePig's distillery manager, introduces their two stills:

In here we do redistillation as well as estate distillation. For redistillation, we're running primarily on Mortimer. For our estate distillation, we run on Mauve. Our estate distillation is what we're really proud of here and what we're trying to expand. It's that stuff where we grow 100 percent on the farm, do traditional mashing, ferment for three days and 100 percent of the ferment goes in. For our redistillation, we redistill imported product from Canada on top of grain. We're trying to add more of our grain into our redistilled products. We're trying to move towards more and more of our estate product.

Peter adds:

Mortimer is the name of one of our stills in here. We love pigs around here. Mortimer was one of our pig mascots back in the day. We had show pigs, these potbelly pigs. We took them around the country to sales events. It really worked as a sales tool, but it also endeared the pigs to our hearts. When they unfortunately passed away over the years, we would dedicate things to them. Mortimer is one of our stills. The Spirit of Mortimer is one of the Boss Hogs. The Mauve was Mortimer's lover and is the name of a still and was last year's Boss Hog. They actually have a love child named Mortimer Junior, and that's our baby still right there.

WhistlePig's substantial aged inventory is housed onsite at the farm and across the border in New York.

The reason for that is that Vermont severely limits the amount of barrels that we can have in the state, period. I think they limit it to 1,500 on site and 4,000 off site. We own about 30,000 to 40,000 barrels,

WhistlePig stays true to its namesake with a pedigree of porcine mascots. *Courtesy of WhistlePig Whiskey.*

so that doesn't work for us. We built this warehouse across the lake in Moriah, New York. It's a nice way for us to grow the business, because we're contract warehousing. We're building more than we need now, knowing we'll need it in the future, and using the space for those who have immediate needs. Various brands tend to live in our warehouses for some amount of time. It may become a bottling or blending facility at some point in time as well.

Peter has a wealth of knowledge regarding aging and maturation chemistry, and one could easily spend a day talking to him about the subject.

We don't do a regular barrel treatment. We do a toast and char profile. So I'll see what our toast and char profile on our Vermont oak gives us on a graph versus what I'd see on regular oak. Flavor compounds like eugenol—these sort of darker, heavier flavors, mocha notes, spice notes. Not tannins, per se, but these structural compounds are going to peak a bit more. More intensity. It depends on the heat treatment of the barrel. Higher heat treatment will destroy more vanillin, etc. Barrels are not apples to apples, when it comes down to it.

Not all barrels are created equal. The same could be said about rye whiskey.

> *We lucked out that the resurgence of rye was hand in hand with the resurgence of the cocktail movement. Every time I do a tasting, I go through what rye whiskey is. You never know; half the people in the room may have no idea. Lighter, floral, grassy…caramel, vanillins and oak tannin—that's one of the things you'll find in our products. We strive to show the different sides of rye.*

WILD HART DISTILLERY

Craig Stevens: *Owner*
Joe Buswell: *Head Distiller*

Craig Stevens, owner of Wild Hart Distillery, speaks with a twinkle in his eye:

> *We're kind of a pirate ship here. So if you're talking about a wild animal, we're a little bit like that. Maybe you get an inkling that we're not as conventional as other folks. We run a business. We're a little tongue-in-cheek. We're a little self-deprecating. There's definitely an outdoors component, a Vermont component, and definitely our attitudes—we're a little crazed, a little unpredictable, a little unconventional. Which so far seems to work.*[82]

Founded in 2017, Wild Hart Distillery is one of Vermont's newest distilling ventures. Located just south of Burlington in Shelburne, the distillery is situated in the up-and-coming Vermont Artisan Village, a chic industrial park that also houses Scottish bakery Douglas Sweets, Vermont Tortilla Company and Fiddlehead Brewery.

Craig adds:

> *We were incorporated in 2015, so had some time of planning before that. Doors didn't open until November 2017. It's kind of wiggly because the building had to be made. We got this [building] essentially designed how we wanted it. The walls got placed, the tasting room took up the place we needed. We had the sprinklers put in for an added safety component. But*

it took time to build the building. This park has potential, which is one of the reasons we landed here. We got in during the early phase, which has its pros and cons. We still don't have enough folks to create a draw. We're the newest ones. We depend more on bringing folks into this space.

Few people realize the difficulties inherent in designing a production space and bringing a product to market. A solid business plan and delicious product only get you so far. Craig Stevens deftly navigated a series of hurdles to get Wild Hart to where it is today. While doing so, he met head distiller Joe Buswell. A veteran of Vermont's distilling industry, Joe has distilled for several major Vermont producers and has consulted for many others. Craig explains:

Joe literally bailed us out. We went to the TTB with a product and a flavor profile that was fantastic. The guidance we got on the development of it wasn't so hot. It failed the TTB. Looking back on it, we should have known. It wasn't on the list as a generally safe product. It wasn't going to happen. We worked at least six months on a flavor, and then we brought in Joe. "You've got ten runs on the still, make it happen." I think Joe made it happen in five.

Wild Hart Distillery's logo combines nature and a distinctly unique script. *Courtesy of Wild Hart Distillery.*

Wild Hart focuses on producing quality spirits, but Craig believes that the distillery can also become a center for innovation and entrepreneurship.

I'd love to see this building stay as it is and become an innovation center and to have us build a ten-thousand-square-foot facility next door. This is a place where people can come, be trained, have contract distilling done. It's not just that we're going to produce it and slap your label on it. You're going to learn how to do it with an incremental approach to starting a distillery, regardless of how large it is—creating a market, exploring a market. If I had my way, Joe would own this building, getting his innovation center. He'd have a big chair on top of a pallet rack and would sit up there and direct people—Guru Joe.

Craig continues:

I think one of the other elements that was missing overall in terms of types of guidance to get was which still to purchase. It's very difficult to understand—everyone wants to sell a still. Everyone says it's going to be plug and play, but it's not. I think if Joe was involved earlier with the level of knowledge he's got, we'd at least be more prepared and the decision of getting the still would be more informed. It became clear that the technical requirements of the still would exceed my abilities to run it. We didn't put as much down, but Joe spends a lot more time working on it—either modifying it or more time actually running it.

Joe agrees and elaborates on the system:

She's a little fussy. She's like a Jaguar, those fancy cars. A little fussy, you know? My wife might describe me in the same way—generally positive, but a little fussy....It's a three-hundred-gallon system you can do just about anything on. We can go through a sixteen-plate vodka column, but we don't do too much vodka. We've got a four-plate whiskey column, but we're not doing much with whiskey right now. We've put some in barrels. Our focus is gin. When we do gin, we do a vapor path extraction using the gin basket over there. It's pretty far away from the boil, which makes it a little more floral, more gentle I guess.

Gin is a broad category. Common brands like Beefeater, Tanqueray and Bombay Sapphire all fall under the London Dry style, juniper and citrus-forward. Plymouth gin, restricted to production in Plymouth, England, is a touch sweeter and earthier. Genever is an old, malt-forward Dutch spirit—the grandfather of gin, so to speak.

Finally, there is the newer American dry style. Rounder than and not nearly as bright as London dry, American (or Western) dry gin relies less on juniper and more on its supporting cast of botanicals. As they can be crafted in myriad ways, American craft distilleries, in particular, have taken to producing American dry gins as a means of differentiation. For Craig and Wild Hart, the decision to produce an American dry gin has a lot to do with market research and timing.

> *I basically did a lot of research on the types of gins that were out there. I found the American dry style; I don't know if it's still emerging as a style. It's got maybe eight to ten years of development under its belt, and practice usually lags behind research at least ten years. So maybe we're right at the pinnacle or right point where American dry can make some headway. But it's providing us an opportunity to have a unique profile and open up people's eyes to gin. It's something not so dominated by juniper, and it's also—because you're using fewer ingredients, you're able to look at tasting those flavors, mixing against those flavors differently than you would with*

Wild Hart's still may not have the most intuitive design, but it makes up for it with flexibility and output. *Courtesy of Wild Hart Distillery.*

London dry. If you have fifteen ingredients in small amounts, can you really mix against those or do they just get lost?

In addition to the American dry gin, Craig and Joe produce a gin that includes Makrut Lime-Leaf Maple Syrup from Runamok maple in Cambridge, Vermont. They also make Burning Embers, a unique product born in collaboration with Shelburne Vineyards. Craig elaborates on their relationship with the vineyard:

We worked with Shelburne Vineyards to develop a vodka infused with fruit and spices, blending it with their Petite Pearl red wine. We sold through it with zero effort. All right, double the amount that we're making and basically we've run out of Vermont wine. So that's a good thing. There are challenges with the product, but it's a very unique product, and folks seem to be gravitating towards it.

Running a distillery requires as much creativity as it does concrete vision and business sense. That said, not everyone enjoys coming up with labels and product names. Many distilleries opt to label products with generic descriptions, letting their overall brand speak for the spirit. Craig explains:

Logos, names, they're all the shittiest things to do. It's horrible. So our American Dry Gin, that's because it's an American dry style. For Vermont Classic, we did have a marketing person. She asked, "Why did you put maple in it?" "Because that's a classic thing to do in Vermont." "Why don't you just call it that?" And I liked the simplicity of it. Burning Embers, the wine-vodka, is built off a Swedish glogg recipe, and burning embers is an old translation of glogg.

The name Wild Hart itself is an exploration of identity, of knowing who you are and owning your image. A delightful play on words, the distillery's name speaks to a free spirit, a spirit as wild as the hills of Vermont. Craig continues:

Wild Hart is a spinoff of, "Well, what are you drinking?" "The hearts of it." And this goes to my rudimentary creativity. You want to speak to the concept of hearts, but you don't want it to be H-E-A-R-T. Wild Heart, like a sixteen-year-old writing on my notebook. Craig "Wild Heart" Joe, you know? An alternative: a hart is a red deer, which to me speaks to the super-outdoors. You might not be normal if you got into the industry, but you want to put out an outward face of being polished. And we're like, "Yeah, there are a few dings. And we're okay with showing it. You should be okay with showing it."

Joe laughs. "So that's where the name came from. Can you haiku that shit?"

A deer, a darling:
The Wild Hart Distillery.
Drink Vermont-Made Gin.

Chapter 7

COCKTAIL CULTURE

A Gateway to Vermont Distilleries

C raft cocktails represent an amazing way to showcase local spirits and ingredients, either as part of a classic cocktail or as a uniquely designed expression of visual art, flavor and aroma. Although Vermont is well known for craft beer, cocktails are a relatively new addition to the state's food and beverage scene.

Sam Nelis, president of the Green Mountain chapter of the United States Bartenders' Guild, describes the recent development of cocktail culture in Vermont.[83]

The USBG, the United States Bartenders' Guild, has chapters all around the country in different cities. We petitioned to have one statewide since we're a smaller state, and they allowed us, so we have the Vermont chapter. It's called the Green Mountain chapter of the USBG. We have about seventy members right now, which is on par with some of the bigger metropolitan areas. In Vermont, it was founded about five years ago, but we didn't become incorporated until about two years ago. It's a long process with national, getting the tax information in, becoming an actual organization with a bank account. It puts us on the map, I'd say. At the same time in the last five years, there were great cocktails happening before that. In the last five years, we've become more noticed nationwide. Vermont started getting invited to regional conferences. Larger distributors and spirit companies started coming to Vermont and educating more. Suddenly we were on people's radars. What we don't have in quantity as far as population and bars in general, we have in quality. I think it's that the food and drink movement in Vermont comes more naturally than in other spaces.[84]

The following section features cocktail recipes from Vermont distilleries and bartenders, a spirited group of individuals dedicated to the cultivation of a thriving cocktail culture and the appreciation of quality beverages. Enjoy!

• • •

Barrelhead Old Fashioned
Old Route Two Distillery

¼ ounce cold water
1 teaspoon maple syrup
4 dashes aromatic bitters
1 lemon twist
1 large ice cube
2 ounces Old Route Two Maple & Ash Barrelhead Rum
1 orange twist

Assemble in a rocks glass. Muddle together water, maple syrup, bitters and the lemon twist. Add the ice cube and Maple & Ash Barrelhead Rum. Stir until combined. Twist the orange over the glass to express the essential oils, then wipe the rim of the glass before dropping the orange twist into the drink.

• • •

The Bee's Knees
Caledonia Spirits

2 ounces Barr Hill Gin
¾ ounce fresh lemon juice
¾ ounce raw honey syrup (2:1)
Lemon twist garnish

Combine ingredients in a mixing tin, add ice, shake, then double strain into a chilled cocktail glass. Add garnish.

• • •

Benton Park Swizzle
Mad River Distillers

1 ½ ounces First Run Rum
¾ ounce simple syrup
¾ ounce lime juice
Mint leaves
¼ ounce Fernet Branca

Put rum, simple syrup and lime juice in a shaker with 4 mint leaves and ice and shake hard. Strain into an ice-filled glass and float Fernet Branca on top. Garnish with a mint leaf.

• • •

Cranberry Cracked Pepper Fizz
Old Route Two Distillery

1 ½ ounces Old Route Two Joe's Pond Gin
1 ounce Vermont Village Cranberry Sipping Vinegar
¼ ounce Sumptuous Syrups Yellow Ginger
Fresh cracked black pepper
Club soda

Combine all ingredients except club soda. Shake over ice, strain into rocks glass over ice and top off with club soda.

• • •

Cucumber Vesper
SILO Distillery

2 ounces SILO Gin
¾ ounce SILO Cucumber Vodka
¼ ounce Lillet Blanc
Lime zest garnish

Shake ingredients with ice for 10 seconds. Strain into a chilled cocktail glass. Squeeze zest over drink and drop remainder into the glass.

• • •

The Customs House
Old Route Two Distillery

1 ½ ounces Coffee Rum
1 dash smoked chili bitters
4 ounces hot cocoa

Add rum and bitters to hot cocoa, stir and serve. For a fun twist, add some whipped cream to the top and sprinkle with ground coffee or cinnamon.

• • •

Distiller's Choice Monte Carlo
WhistlePig Whiskey

2 ounces WhistlePig ten-year, 100-proof Rye Whiskey
½ ounce Benedictine
2 dashes Angostura bitters

Fill mixing glass with ice and add all ingredients. Stir until very chilled and strain into a rocks glass over a large ice cube.

• • •

East of Toronto
SILO Distillery

2 ounces SILO Whiskey
½ ounce Zucca (rhubarb amaro)
½ ounce simple syrup
2 dashes rhubarb bitters
Orange twist

Stir ingredients with ice. Strain over a large ice cube into a rocks glass or serve up in a cocktail glass. Garnish with orange twist.

• • •

First Love
Stonecutter Spirits

1 ½ ounces Stonecutter Spirits Heritage Cask Whiskey
¾ ounce Aperol
½ ounce lemon juice
¼ ounce maple syrup
1 dash Angostura bitters
Club soda, to top

Mix ingredients in a glass with ice. Top with club soda. Serve.

• • •

Flying Crow Espresso Martini
House cocktail by Copper Fox, Springfield, Vermont

1 ½ ounces SILO Vodka
¾ ounce Courvoisier v.s.o.p.
¾ ounce Mr. Black Coffee Liqueur
¾ ounce Bailey's Irish Cream
½ ounce freshly brewed Flying Crow Espresso, chilled

Shake ingredients with ice, strain with a strainer and allow foam to pass into a chilled martini glass. Garnish with 3 coffee beans.

• • •

Hell's Gate Kir
Hell's Gate Distillery

1 ½ ounces Black Pearl Black Currant Liqueur
¾ ounce Regal Onyx Black Currant Brandy
Vermont hard apple cider
Black currant or berry garnish

Pour the Black Pearl and Regal Onyx into a champagne flute. Top slowly with hard cider. Garnish with black currant or berries.

• • •

Herb Tail
WhistlePig Whiskey

2 ounces WhistlePig ten-year, 100-proof Rye Whiskey
¾ ounce Galliano
4 dashes Fernet

Build in a mixing glass. Fill mixing glass with ice and stir. Strain in a chilled cocktail glass.

• • •

Light Spanking
Wild Hart Distillery

2 ounces American dry gin
4 ounces grapefruit juice
½ ounce Rose Petal Simple Syrup**
Large sprig of rosemary
Lemon wheel for garnish

Combine all parts in Boston shaker. Add ice and shake vigorously. Pour into rocks glass. Garnish with lemon wheel.
** For Rose Petal Simple Syrup, dissolve 1 cup of sugar in 1 cup of water. Reduce to a simmer and add 2 cups of fresh, edible rose petals (1 cup dried). Simmer for 10 minutes, remove from heat and steep for 10 minutes. Strain and chill.

• • •

Maple Rum-hattan
St. Johnsbury Distillery

2 ounces Dunc's Maple Rum
1 ounce sweet vermouth
2 dashes Angostura bitters
Lime peel
Ice

In a rocks glass with ice, stir rum, vermouth and bitters. Twist a lime peel, rim the glass and drop the peel in.

• • •

Maple White Russian
Vermont Distillers

2 ounces Metcalfe's Vermont Maple Cream Liqueur
1 ounce Catamount Vodka
½ ounce coffee liqueur

Shake ingredients, pour over ice and serve.

• • •

The Marshfield
Hooker Mountain Farm Distillery

1 ½ ounces Hooker Mountain Farm Bourbon Mash Whiskey
1 ½ ounces Hooker Mountain Farm Spirited Cider
Freshly pitted cherries

Shake whiskey and Spirited Cider for 10 seconds, until cold. Serve in your favorite glass, garnished with a cherry.

• • •

The Montpelier
Old Route Two Distillery

2 ounces Old Route Two Cherrywood Barrelhead Rum
1 ounce sweet vermouth
Dash Angostura bitters
Dash orange bitters
Cherry for garnish

Assemble in a rocks glass. Stir with a large ice cube and serve garnished with a cherry.

• • •

The Quill (a variation on a classic Negroni)
Appalachian Gap Distillery

1 ½ ounces Mythic Gin
1 ounce Campari
1 ounce Carpano Antica
¼ ounce Absinthe
Orange peel for garnish

Combine all ingredients in a shaker with ice. Shake. Strain into a chilled glass. Garnish with an orange peel.

• • •

Resting Spritz Face
Wild Hart Distillery

1 ounce Wild Hart Burning Embers
2 ounces prosecco
2 ounces ginger beer
Orange slice for garnish

Mix all ingredients over ice and serve garnished with an orange slice.

• • •

Rhuby Tuesday
Smugglers' Notch Distillery

1 ½ ounces Smugglers' Notch Distillery Gin
1 ounce Boyden Valley Winery Rhubarb Wine
½ ounce fresh lemon juice
⅓ ounce Sumptuous Syrups Black Currant
Sea salt/sugar rim (1:1 ratio)
Cherry garnish

Combine gin, rhubarb wine, lemon and Sumptuous Black Currant Syrup in shaker with ice. Shake vigorously. Strain into sea salt/sugar rimmed cocktail glass or coupe. Add cherry garnish.

• • •

Rock, Paper, Scissor
Stonecutter Spirits

¾ ounce Stonecutter Spirits Heritage Cask Whiskey
¾ ounce Averna amaro
¾ ounce Aperol
¾ ounce lemon juice

Vigorously stir ingredients with ice. Strain over a large ice cube in a rocks glass or serve up in a coupe or martini glass.

• • •

Royalty Is Overrated
SILO Distillery

1 ounce SILO Vodka
½ ounce triple sec
Lemonade
1 ounce Chambord, chilled
Dram black bitters
Black raspberry garnish

Shake vodka, triple sec and lemonade with ice. Strain into a martini glass. Pour the chilled Chambord down the side of the glass so it settles at the bottom. Add a dash of bitters and garnish with black raspberry.

• • •

Shelburne Sidecar
Shelburne Orchards Distillery

1 ounce Dead Bird Apple Brandy
1 ounce Cointreau
1 ounce freshly squeezed lemon juice
Orange peel twist, for garnish

Fill a cocktail shaker halfway with ice cubes. Add the Calvados, Cointreau and lemon juice. Shake well, then strain into a glass. Garnish with an orange twist.

• • •

Sippin' on Gin and Spruce
Hooker Mountain Farm Distillery

Swirl of maple syrup
2 ounces Spruce Gin
½ ounce freshly squeezed lime juice
Seltzer water
Lime garnish

Swirl a glass with maple syrup. Add ice. Shake gin and lime juice, strain into glass and top with seltzer water. Garnish with a lime wedge.

• • •

Smugglers' Punch
Smugglers' Notch Distillery

3 ounces Smugglers' Notch Bourbon Barrel–Aged Rum
1 ounce lime juice
1 ounce lemon juice
6 ounces orange juice
2 teaspoons sugar
Dash of grenadine syrup

Combine all ingredients into a Boston shaker containing ice. Shake until well frosted and strain into a glass containing ice.

• • •

Spicy Henry
Wild Hart Distillery

½ ounce lemon juice
1 ounce honey simple syrup (1:1 ratio)
3 slices jalapeño pepper
2 ounces Wild Hart Vermont Classic Gin

Combine lemon juice, honey and jalapeño in a cocktail shaker. Muddle ingredients. Add gin and ice. Shake and strain into chilled martini glass. Garnish with lemon peel and jalapeño.

• • •

Stonecutter Negroni
Stonecutter Spirits

2 ounces Stonecutter Spirits Single-Barrel Gin
½ ounce Campari
¼ ounce sweet vermouth
¼ ounce dry vermouth
2 dashes orange bitters

In a rocks glass, stir ingredients with a large ice cube. Serve.

• • •

Sugarbush Saddle
Smugglers' Notch Distillery

2 ounces Smugglers' Notch Distillery Straight Bourbon Whiskey
2 dashes Urban Moonshine Maple Bitters
½ ounce Sumptuous Syrups Yellow Ginger
Soda water
1 long, wide lemon peel

In a Collins glass, combine bourbon, bitters and yellow ginger syrup. Add lemon peel, ice and soda. Stir and enjoy.

• • •

Summer in Vermont
WhistlePig Whiskey

Fresh blackberries
Fresh mint
¾ ounce fresh lemon juice
½ ounce WhistlePig Maple Syrup
2 ounces WhistlePig ten-year, 100-proof Rye Whiskey

Add blackberries, mint and maple syrup to a mix tin and muddle. Add fresh lemon juice and dry shake. Add WhistlePig ten-year and ice, shake until cold. Double strain over a large cube of ice in a rocks glass. Garnish with fresh mint sprigs and a fresh blackberry on a stick.

• • •

Vermont and Stormy
Saxtons River Distillery

1 ½ ounces Sapling Maple Liqueur
4 ounces ginger beer
Slice of lime

Fill glass with ice, add ingredients and stir gently.

• • •

Vermont Harvest
Saxtons River Distillery

1 lemon wedge
2–3 fresh sage leaves
3–4 fresh tarragon leaves
2½ ounces Sapling Maple Bourbon
Ginger beer

Muddle lemon and herbs. Add Sapling Maple Bourbon and shake vigorously with ice. Strain into chilled martini glass, top with ginger beer and garnish with lemon zest.

• • •

Vieux Montpelier
circa 2019 Sam Nelis, Caledonia Spirits

1 ounce Montpelier Tom Cat Gin
1 ounce Mad River Distillers Mad Apple Brandy
1 ounce sweet vermouth
1 teaspoon Benedictine
2 dashes Angostura bitters
2 dashes Peychaud's bitters
Orange twist and cherry for garnish

Combine ingredients in a mixing glass, add ice, stir and then strain over fresh ice in old fashioned glass and garnish with an orange twist and cherry flag.

(The classic Vieux Carre cocktail was created circa 1937 by Walter Bergeron at the famous Carousel bar in the Hotel Monteleone in New Orleans. Our version is an ode to the capital city of Vermont and the location of our new distillery and cocktail bar, now open!)

• • •

WhistlePig Maple Old Fashioned
100 percent WhistlePig-owned cocktail

2 ounces WhistlePig ten-year, 100-proof Rye Whiskey
¼ ounce WhistlePig Barrel-Aged Maple Syrup
4 dashes WhistlePig Maple Bitters
Orange peel for garnish

Add rye whiskey, maple syrup and maple bitters to a rocks glass. Add a large ice cube. Stir until maple syrup is fully dissolved. Garnish with an orange peel.

Chapter 8

CLOSING THOUGHTS

B y the time this book is released, much of the data represented herein will be outdated. Our industry moves quickly, as did the beer and wine industries before us. Will the Vermont spirits industry change? Absolutely. We see new DSPs launch every year and, unfortunately, recently saw our first closing. Legislation is an ongoing battle at both the federal and state levels, sometimes resulting in a great victory but just as frequently creating pitfalls and setbacks.

I consider myself lucky to have met most of the distillery owners in the state, even luckier to call many of them friends. They're good people, honest, doing their best to sustain and grow hard-fought businesses. That's not to say that some don't play their cards close to their chests. Individuals come into distilling from all walks of life: farming, sales, upper management, academia, laboratories. Many producers are refreshingly transparent, but in some cases, old habits die hard.

I'm perhaps most frequently asked if market saturation is imminent. Based on American Craft Spirits Association projections, I'd wager we're far from it. Bartenders and wholesalers alike believe that craft spirits are not only here to stay but will continue to carve out large sections of the market, perhaps even eclipsing beer and wine. Due to our small population, Vermont will likely continue to boast the largest number of producing distilleries per capita, as it does with breweries.

Maybe some of Vermont's distilleries will make the jump from regional powerhouses to national or international staples; a couple are already on the doorstep. It will be interesting to see what those in the second wave of distilleries in Vermont—those coming online now—do with the roads that have already been paved. Compared to the first wave of entrepreneurs, for many of whom distilling was a second or third career, several new manufacturers will enter the market after apprenticing or working for established producers. We've seen it with brewing, and we'll see it with spirits as well. Whatever happens, for whatever reason, I take comfort knowing that our cocktails will be well crafted, our rocks glasses filled and that the future of spirits in Vermont is as certain as our mountains are green and our powder is fresh.

Sláinte!

ABOUT THE DISTILLED SPIRITS COUNCIL OF VERMONT

The Distilled Spirits Council of Vermont is a cooperative, nonprofit organization created to develop, promote and maintain the distilled spirits industry in Vermont. The council members provide the region and tourists with the farm-to-table experience that Vermont is known for, while focusing their support on the regional craft distilling industry.

Funding for the Distilled Spirits Council of Vermont website is provided by the Vermont Agricultural Innovation Center.

www.distilledvermont.org

NOTES

Introduction

1. Allchin, "India."
2. Pastis is an anise- and licorice-flavored spirit similar to the likes of ouzo, sambuca, arak and raki. Common to southern France, it is typically diluted with water when consumed.
3. According to the American Craft Spirits Association, there were 656 craft distilleries in 2013. In August 2018, there were 1,835 distilleries.
4. The United States Census Bureau reports that Vermont's population was estimated at 626,299 in 2018. Of all fifty states and Washington, D.C., only Wyoming has a smaller population.

Chapter 1

5. Lazor, "Brief History of Grain."
6. Gleason and Gleason, "Growing Wheat in Vermont."
7. Lazor, "Brief History of Grain."
8. Peterson, interview with the author. Unless otherwise noted, all quotes in this chapter are from this interview.
9. Jeff delivered grain to SILO in a small box truck, ten thousand pounds at a time. He and I would unload the truck by hand, fifty-pound sack at a time. Andrew delivered in a pickup truck, also unloaded by hand. Deliveries are tough for farmers, who already work long hours and need to spend considerable time with

their crops. As such, deliveries represent a significant obstacle to the inclusion of local and regional ingredients at the scale necessary for distillation.

10. Lazor, "Brief History of Grain."
11. Caledonia Spirits, "Our Story."

Chapter 2

12. For most of my career as a distiller, I've operated without a forklift. Crazy, I know, but unloading ten thousand pounds of grain, fifty-pound sack at a time, is a great way to save money on a gym membership. Carrying them up a six-foot ladder to empty them into a mill does a number on calves, triceps, lats and traps. Dust from grain sacks quickly settles on hair, skin and clothes. So much for looking nice!
13. Marcotte, "Distilling Milling Efficiency."
14. Russell and Stewart, *Whiskey*, 88–93.
15. Ibid., 72–79.
16. Gelatinization temperatures vary depending on the specifics of the grain and the methods of analysis, resulting in broad and diverse temperature ranges.
17. Esters and congeners are responsible for flavors including caramel, butterscotch, banana, green apple, smokiness, almond, vanilla and much more.
18. Technology and instruments, while useful, are not necessary to produce a good product. Distillers can be trained to operate exclusively using sensory data, but gauges, alarms and probes make the process safer and more consistent between users.

Chapter 3

19. Twede, "Cask Age."
20. Klein, *Science of Measurement*, 32–38.
21. Thanks to the brewing, winemaking and distilling industries, coopering is experiencing a resurgence in the United States. The machinery and materials required to start a cooperage are costly, and scale is an important factor. Local and regional woods are unproven and untested, making the use of locally supplied barrels a risky proposition.
22. Fletcher and Broich, personal communication with author. Unless otherwise noted, all quotes in this chapter are from this interview.
23. TTB, "Class and Type Designation," chapter 4.
24. Buxton and Hughes, *Science and Commerce of Whiskey*, 147–48.
25. Russell and Stewart, *Whiskey*, 202–8.
26. Buxton and Hughes, *Science and Commerce of Whiskey*, 148–49.

27. TTB, "Class and Type Designation," Chapter 4.
28. Russell and Stewart, *Whiskey*, 213–15.
29. Based on the author's experiences and conversations with distillers using small-format barrels.

Chapter 4

30. Label and recipe submissions are usually completed online. Once submitted, users will receive notification of acceptance, rejection or needs-to-correct. The TTB publishes an expected wait time for responses.
31. TTB, "What You Should Know About Distilled Spirits Labels."
32. Ibid.
33. Vermont Agency of Commerce and Community Development, "Leveraging the Vermont Brand."
34. Ibid.
35. Ibid.
36. Nelis, personal communication with author.
37. Elliott, personal communication with author.
38. Christiansen, personal communication with author.
39. Cotel, personal communication with author.
40. The National Alcoholic Beverage Control Association (NABCA) maintains a control state directory and information on each state's makeup and sales.

Chapter 5

41. Vermont has a long and storied past regarding the prohibition of beverage alcohol. It became the nation's second dry state in 1853, long before the period of national Prohibition. During this period, Vermont's proximity to Canada encouraged widespread smuggling, bootlegging and other alcohol-related crimes.
42. Delaney, personal communication with author. Unless otherwise noted, all quotes in this chapter are from this interview.
43. NABCA, "Control State Directory and Info."
44. New Hampshire's FY 2016 Net Revenue was $156,000,000. Since its first store opened in 1934, New Hampshire has raised over $3 billion in net profits.
45. Jeremy Elliott explores some of DSCVT's successes in the foreword of this book. Not every Vermont distillery belongs to the DSCVT.
46. Christiansen, personal communication with author.
47. Hughes, personal communication with author.
48. Cotel, personal communication with author.

Chapter 6

49. Burkins and Hubbard, personal communication with author. Unless otherwise noted, all quotes in this chapter are from this interview.

50. As temperatures rise and fall, the contents of a barrel expand and contract. This creates a "breathing" of sorts, which forces the spirit to enter and retract from the wood.

51. Christiansen, personal communication with author. Unless otherwise noted, all quotes in this chapter are from this interview.

52. Vermont has its own versions of romantic Prohibition stories. Line houses straddled the Vermont and Canada border. Visitors could enter via the Vermont side and proceed through the house to the Canadian side, where a bar could legally serve alcohol.

53. Gagner and Kehaya, personal communication with author. Unless otherwise noted, all quotes in this chapter are from this interview.

54. St. Hilaire and St. Hilaire, personal communication with author. Unless otherwise noted, all quotes in this chapter are from this interview.

55. I've tried making grappa. It's not easy. Working with grape pomace is laborious and tedious. The grape solids are difficult to transport, and it is easy to over-extract too many vegetal flavors. My R&D trials tasted like overripe bell peppers rather than brandy!

56. Randolph and Randolph, personal communication with author,. Unless otherwise noted, all quotes in this chapter are from this interview.

57. Fernet refers to a group of spirits in the amaro family, a classification of digestive liquors known for a complex botanical build and sharp, medicinal bitterness.

58. Irish poitín, pronounced *PUUT-cheen*, is a traditional Irish spirit distilled from cereals, grain, whey, sugar beet molasses and potatoes in a manner similar to whiskey.

59. Hilton, personal communication with author. Unless otherwise noted, all quotes in this section are from this interview.

60. Dumperth and Overbay, personal communication with author. Unless otherwise noted, all quotes in this section are from this interview.

61. Small R&D nano-stills are commonplace among craft distillers. They can be invaluable when developing new products, allowing manufacturers the chance to finetune recipes. As with any recipe construction, distillers must be careful when scaling up from a small distillation—ingredient utilization, efficiency and other aspects of the spirit will change as equipment changes.

62. Stromberg, personal communication with author. Unless otherwise noted, all quotes in this section are from this interview.

63. Cowles, personal communication with author. Unless otherwise noted, all quotes in this section are from this interview.

64. Jillson, personal communication with author.

65. Ibid.

66. Bell, personal communication with author.

67. Ibid.

68. Ibid.

69. Jillson, personal communication with author.

70. Bell, personal communication with author.

71. Elliott, personal communication with author. Unless otherwise noted, all quotes in this section are from this interview.

72. Hughes and Hughes, personal communication with author. Unless otherwise noted, all quotes in this section are from this interview.

73. Holaday, personal communication with author.

74. Ibid.

75. Ibid.

76. Cotel, personal communication with author. Unless otherwise noted, all quotes in this section are from this interview.

77. Ed Metcalfe, personal communication with author, January 17, 2019. Unless otherwise noted, all quotes in this section are from this interview.

78. Calta, "Maverick Distillers in Vermont."

79. Johnson, personal communication with author. Unless otherwise noted, all quotes in this section are from this interview.

80. Lynch and Harrison, personal communication with author. Unless otherwise noted, all quotes in this section are from this interview.

81. WhistlePig's master distiller, Dave Pickerell, passed away in November 2018. A legend in the industry, he was pivotal in the growth of Maker's Mark bourbon and was known as a founding father of craft distilling. In addition to his work at WhistlePig, Pickerell consulted for over one hundred spirits companies and served for a period as the master distiller for the restored George Washington's Distillery in Mount Vernon, Virginia.

82. Stevens and Buswell, personal communication with author. Unless otherwise noted, all quotes in this section are from this interview.

Chapter 7

83. Nelis, personal communication with author.

84. Vermont's chapter of the USBG hosts a statewide cocktail competition each year. The competition is heavily supported by members of the Distilled Spirits Council of Vermont and Vermont's distilling community at-large.

BIBLIOGRAPHY

Alcohol and Tobacco Tax and Trade Bureau. "Class and Type Designation." April 2007.

————. "What You Should Know About Distilled Spirits." April 2008.

Allchin, F.R. "India: The Ancient Home of Distillation?" *Man, New Series*, 1979.

American Craft Spirits Association. "Craft Spirits Data Project." 2018.

Bell, Erin. Interview by Chris Maggiolo. May 27, 2019.

Burkins, Chuck, and Lars Hubbard. Interview by Chris Maggiolo. November 15, 2018.

Buxton, Ian, and Paul S. Hughes. *The Science and Commerce of Whiskey.* Cambridge, UK: RSC Publishing, 2014.

Caledonia Spirits. "Our Story." 2019. caledoniaspirits.com/our-story.

Calta, MariaLisa. "Maverick Distillers in Vermont Produce Maple Syrup with a Kick." February 15, 1989. www.nytimes.com.

Christiansen, Ryan. Interview by Chris Maggiolo. April 23, 2019.

Cotel, Sivan. Interview by Chris Maggiolo. November 15, 2018.

Cowles, Nick. Interview by Chris Maggiolo. April 21, 2019.

Delaney, Patrick. Interview by Chris Maggiolo. April 23, 2019.

Distilled Spirits Council of the United States. 2019. www.distilledspirits.org.

Distilled Spirits Council of Vermont. 2019. www.distilledvermont.org.

Dumperth, Ryan, and Adam Overbay. Interview by Chris Maggiolo. February 7, 2019.

Elliott, Jeremy. Interview by Chris Maggiolo. March 14, 2019.

Fletcher, Tony, and Mac Broich. Interview by Chris Maggiolo. April 11, 2019.

Gagner, Steve, and Matt Kehaya. Interview by Chris Maggiolo. April 24, 2019.

Gleason, Ben, and Theresa Gleason. "Growing Wheat in Vermont." northerngraingrowers.org.

Hilton, Alex. Interview by Chris Maggiolo. February 7, 2019.

Holaday, Duncan. Interview by Chris Maggiolo. May 2, 2019.

Hughes, Brendan, and Dan Hughes. Interview by Chris Maggiolo. May 2, 2019.

Jillson, Peter. Interview by Chris Maggiolo. April 29, 2019.

Johnson, Steve. Interview by Chris Maggiolo. May 3, 2019.

Klein, Herbert Arthur. *The Science of Measurement: A Historical Survey.* New York: Dover Publications, 1974.

Krakowski, Adam. *Vermont Prohibition: Teetotalers, Bootleggers, & Corruption.* Charleston, SC: The History Press, 2016.

Lazor, Jack. "A Brief History of Grain Production in Vermont: Part One." northerngraingrowers.org.

Lynch, Peter, and Emily Harrison. Interview by Chris Maggiolo. April 24, 2019.

Marcotte, Eric. "Distilling Milling Efficiency." www.stedman-machine.com/distillery-milling-efficiency.html.

Metcalfe, Ed. Interview by Chris Maggiolo. January 17, 2019.

National Alcoholic Beverage Control Association. "Analytics & Statistical Data." 2019. www.nabca.org/analytics-statistical-data.

Nelis, Sam. Interview by Chris Maggiolo. May 2, 2019.

Peterson, Andrew. Interview by Chris Maggiolo. April 7, 2019.

Randolph, Kempton, and Carrie Randolph. Interview by Chris Maggiolo. April 23, 2019.

Russell, Inge, and Graham Stewart. *Whiskey: Technology, Production and Marketing.* Oxford: Academic Press, 2014.

Sandomir, Richard. "Dave Pickerell, Master of Whiskey and Rye, Is Dead at 62." *New York Times*, November 9, 2018, B11.

Stevens, Craig, and Joe Buswell. Interview by Chris Maggiolo. April 21, 2019.

St. Hilaire, Judi, and Joe St. Hilaire. Interview by Chris Maggiolo. April 24, 2019.

Stromberg, Christian. Interview by Chris Maggiolo. January 17, 2019.

Twede, Diana. "The Cask Age: The Technology and History of Wooden Barrels." *Packaging Technology and Science*, 2005: 253–64.

United States Bartenders' Guild. 2019. www.usbg.org/home.

United States Census Bureau. 2019. www.census.gov.

Vermont Agency of Commerce and Community Development. "Leveraging the Vermont Brand." 2010.

Vermont Department of Liquor and Lottery. Division of Liquor Control. 2019. liquorcontrol.vermont.gov.

INDEX

A

angel's share 35
Anheuser-Busch 117
Appalachian Gap Distillery 20, 49
apple cider 116
apples 20, 77, 89, 92, 96
Artisans Park 93

B

barley 18, 69
barrel-aging. *See* maturation
barrels
  and oak 33
  charring of 31, 34
  from Vermont oak 34
  history of 29
  production of 30
bottling 36
bourbon 24, 62, 76
  maple bourbon 86, 100
brandy 20, 24, 67, 77, 89, 119
Burlington 112, 116

C

Cabot (town) 68
Caledonia Spirits 20, 53

cocktails
  barrel-aged 120
  culture of 39, 132
collaboration
  with craft breweries 77
contract distilling 87, 128
control state
  and Vermont distillers 44
  goal of 44
  Vermont and New Hampshire 44
  versus licensee state 43
cooperage 30, 150
corn 18, 69, 95
cottage industry 21, 73
craft distillery 25, 38, 48
currants 64
cuts 26
  foreshots 26
  heads 26
  hearts 27
  tails 27

D

Danger Close Craft Distilling 60
distillation 24, 25, 51
  finish run 26
  history of 68

stripping run 26
Distilled Spirits Council of Vermont 39, 45, 100
distilled spirits plants (DSPs) 100
distribution 38, 59
DLC (Division of Liquor Control) 38, 71
DLL (Department of Liquor and Lottery) 44
Dunc's Mill 102, 105

E

education 101, 128
employees 50, 59
estate distillery 120

F

farm distillery 63, 68, 120
farm-to-glass 18, 56, 66, 96, 121
14th Star Brewing Company 60

G

gin 24, 28, 52, 57, 71, 79, 96, 100, 119, 128
    American dry 86, 129
    barrel-aged gin 59, 110
Good Food Awards 110
grain 16, 22
    malting process 17
grapes 64
grappa 65, 67, 152
Green Mountain Grain & Barrel 30, 61, 97
Grembowicz Farm 18
Groennfell Meadery 20

H

Hardwick 53
Hell's Gate Distillery 64
Highball Social 112
Holaday, Duncan 51, 65, 102, 104, 105, 117, 118
honey 20, 57, 58

Hooker Mountain Farm Distillery 68
hops 77

J

Jeffersonville 98
juniper 15, 21, 52, 57, 79, 81, 86, 96, 118, 128, 129

K

krupnikas 85

L

labeling 36, 151
legislation 46
limoncello 116
low wines 26, 51, 95

M

Mad River Distillers 21, 74
maple cream liqueur 115
maple syrup 19, 62, 76, 85, 95, 107, 114, 118
marketing 38, 59, 130
    the Vermont brand 38, 39, 40, 41, 73, 97
Marlboro 114
mash 22, 23
maturation 29, 51, 81, 96
    and barrel size 35, 96
    and climate 113, 152
    and color 33
    and evaporation 34
    and flavor 33, 110, 125
    and oxidation 34
    state limitations 124
Middlebury 49, 108
milling 22

N

North River Winery 114

O

oak 33
  Vermont-grown 34, 121, 122
oats 69
Old Route Two Spirits 20, 78

P

Peterson, Andrew 16, 95
Peterson Quality Malt 16, 21, 95, 96
Pickerell, Dave 123, 153
pommeau 89
potatoes 69
production
  process of 50, 54, 74, 80, 90, 95,
    105, 150
Prohibition 43, 89, 151, 152
proofing 27

Q

Quechee 117

R

rectified spirits 115
rum 24, 76, 79, 107
rye (grain) 18, 95
rye whiskey 24, 77, 121

S

safety 87
San Francisco International Spirit
    Awards 110
Saxtons River Distillery 19, 84
scotch 24
Shelburne 126
Shelburne Orchards Distillery 21, 88
SILO Distillery 21, 93
single malt whiskey 77, 96
Smugglers' Notch Distillery 98, 116
social outreach 62
Springmore Farm 95
St. Albans 60
still 24, 128

column still 24
hybrid still 25, 95, 128
pot still 54, 74
vacuum still 87
St. Johnsbury 102
St. Johnsbury Distillery 102
Stonecutter Spirits 108
sustainability 51, 112

T

tequila 52
terroir 113, 121
Trident Stills 83, 101
TTB (Alcohol and Tobacco Tax and
    Trade Bureau) 36, 104, 119, 127

U

USBG (United States Bartenders'
    Guild) 39, 132

V

Vermont
  state seal 15
Vermont Distillers 19, 114
Vermont Distillers (first distillery in
    Vermont) 116
Vermont Spirits 117
vodka 24, 27, 52, 96, 100, 118
  garlic vodka 116

W

Waitsfield 75
Waterbury 116
wheat 15, 18, 95
whey 71, 107, 119
whiskey 28, 52, 62, 72, 76, 111, 121
WhistlePig Whiskey 108, 120
Wild Hart Distillery 126
Windsor 93

Y

yeast 23

ABOUT THE AUTHOR

C hris Maggiolo's passion for beverages began with the study of rum and herbal remedies in the Caribbean and has since spanned careers in wine, beer and distilled spirits. He holds a BA in anthropology and environmental policy from the College of William and Mary and an MLA in gastronomy from Boston University. Having worked as head distiller of SILO Distillery and as a consultant for distilleries in the northeastern United States and Canada, he currently serves as campus manager of the Black River Innovation Campus in Springfield, Vermont. A native of Virginia, Chris now happily resides in Weathersfield, Vermont with his wife, Laura, and their American foxhound, Barbarella.